PC
372.6
SWA

Swain, Sherry Seale

I can write what's on my
mind: Theresa finds her voice

DATE DUE

I Can Write What's on My Mind

I Can Write What's on My Mind: Theresa Finds Her Voice

Sherry Seale Swain

National Writing Project
Berkeley, California

National Writing Project, Graduate School of Education,
615 University Hall, University of California,
Berkeley, CA 94720.
Telephone 510-642-0963
Fax 510-642-4545

Library of Congress Cataloging-in-Progress

Swain, Sherry Seale, 1946-
    I can write what's on my mind: Theresa finds her voice /
Sherry Seale Swain.
        p.   cm. – (Writing teachers at work; no. 2)
        ISBN 1-883920-09-4
    1. Language arts (Elementary) – Mississippi – Case studies.
    2. English language – Composition and exercises –
    Study and teaching (Elementary) – Mississippi – Case
    studies.   I. Title. II. Series.
LB 1576.S93 1994
372.6044–dc20
                                                      94-27872
                                                         CIP

Series Editor: Miriam Ylvisaker

FOREWORD

Just before Christmas, in a little village in northern California, in an artsy shop called Rookie-to Gallery, my eyes landed on something I thought was a kaleidoscope. Having always loved kaleidoscopes, I picked it up and started turning it around. What I noticed was that the shapes changed but the colors didn't. I thought, "A kaleidoscope with no color?" I put it down, picked up another right beside it filled with colored crystals, and it did the usual kaleidoscope thing. I must have looked puzzled as I picked up the first one again. Smiling, the store owner waited for me to glance his way and said, "That's a teleidoscope. It takes on the colors of whatever you are looking at. When you move to a different perspective, you see different colors and shapes."

So I turned around, looked up and down, and looked close up and far away, at a little boy's red and green painted Christmas shirt and out the window at the sky and the huge magnolias. And sure enough, with each different perspective, I saw a generous diversity of shapes and colors and levels of light. When I focused on one place and moved my position closer or farther or moved to a different angle, I saw it differently. The instrument didn't have to be twirled. I had to twirl. And the more I twirled, the more I saw. I knew Sherry's Christmas present had virtually jumped into my hand. Sherry likes to dance, and the more she twirls, the more light and energy come into her life. Dance gives her light and life and energy and perspective and inner vision and vitality and passion.

As a teacher, Sherry dances too. She moves with the rhythm of the children, responding to the beat of their music. She leads and they follow; they lead and she follows. They do circle dances together and line dances together and take turns being in the circle to dance as a "star" one by one. And as they do, they gain perspective on who they are and what reading and writing and responding and experimenting are about. And they dance the dance of learning together.

Over the last eight years, Sherry has had a teleidoscope through which she looked while the children danced. No, not a physical one. But a marvelous teleidoscope called teacher research. After her first National

Writing Project Invitational Summer Institute, Sherry started a teacher research project. She kept a journal on what she was seeing. She looked from close and from far. She looked from many different angles. As she did, she saw the light and colors of the children and of her work as a teacher. She saw where she wanted to focus more energy in dancing the dance. She saw where she wanted to create new movements or practice old ones or vary the rhythm. She saw where she wanted to linger in the long slow turns and invited the children to watch themselves in slow motion and fast motion and to help create the dance. Then in later years she turned her teleidoscope toward the parents. She invited them to join in the seeing.

As Teacher Consultant of the Mississippi State University Writing/Thinking Project and the Mississippi Writing/Thinking Institute (Mississippi's network of National Writing Project sites) for years and now director of the Mississippi State Project, Sherry has been a member of a growing band of teacher researchers who are seeing their own and each others' students and classrooms through the teleidoscope. Together they teach each others' students. Together they learn from their students. The teleidoscope of teacher research in the twirl of the dance feeds us all.

Sandra Price Burkett
Mississippi State Writing Project Network Director

ACKNOWLEDGMENTS

This book has been a labor of love from its inception. To Theresa and her wonderful parents, I owe gratitude, not only for this publication, but for lessons in parenting, cooperation, and faith. I share ownership in this story with many others, including Cindy Leigh who helped me design the study and who said, "Publish it!" I thank my mentor and friend, Sandra Price Burkett, for constant response, insight, and encouragement. Sam Watson spent a weekend reviewing an early draft and giving valuable response. Teacher Consultants who read, marked copy, and helped clarify the instruction include Pat Mitchell, Johnnie Marshall, Johnnie Gibson, Suzanne Thompson, Lois Mauldin, Faye Edwards, Lynette Harris, Dolyene Davis, Grace Morizawa, and others who picked up drafts and left their responses on yellow stickie notes. Thanks to Andrew Bouman and Leonor Rubio for technical assistance.

I must thank the teachers who've asked the hard questions in inservice sessions I've led. They forced me to look at the theory underlying my practices. To Betty Nail, who never grew weary of reading the latest journal entries and who spent many afternoons discussing Theresa's progress after school, I cannot say enough thank yous. Administrators of Starkville Public Schools, Janet Henderson, Larry Box, and the Board of Trustees, have applauded my work in the classroom and the Writing Project. I appreciate Mary Ann Smith's strong quiet support during the review and editing processes. Miriam Ylvisaker has been my editor, my teacher, my gentle encouraging friend. Jim Gray, founder of the National Writing Project, has given me and millions of other teachers an organization that believes in teachers and provides support for teacher research and publications.

INTRODUCTION

Teaching young children gives me energy, invigorates my thinking, and keeps me learning. I see each child not as a person under construction, but as a whole person, complete with personality, talents, and needs. So my curiosity piqued one August morning when a colleague spoke to me about a child in my class. "You have a little girl who transferred from the private academy," she said as we walked across the school playground to take our respective duty posts.

My first grade class that semester was typical of the seventeen first grade classes in our public school, a school that housed first and second grades for the rural university town of Starkville, Mississippi. The twenty-three children in my class ranged from those who had limited life and academic experiences to those who had traveled widely and were already reading and writing. About half of my twelve boys and eleven girls were African-American, half white.

As a member of the Mississippi Writing/Thinking Institute, I belong to a group of teacher researchers who are looking closely at language and learning in our classrooms. I had decided earlier that I wanted to focus on one child, to prepare a case study that would help others and myself understand my classroom and the children in it. I selected for my study the student who had transferred from the private school, where she had been asked to repeat kindergarten "because," as her mother had told me, "she had not mastered phonics." The child's name was Theresa, and when I asked her mother if she would help with the study. she posed the invitation to Theresa's father and then accepted enthusiastically. In this way she and I became real collaborators in Theresa's education. I highlighted entries about Theresa in my classroom journal and shared them with her mother; she sent notes about Theresa's reading and writing experiences at home to me. As the study progressed, Theresa herself became an involved participant, acting as one of my editors when I occasionally asked her to critique my interpretations of her work. The pages that follow chronicle our journey and Theresa's growth in learning to read and write.

AUGUST 15

"My name is Theresa and I like hamburgers," Theresa whispered in the first sharing circle on the green rug that would become the heart of our classroom. On the second round of the circle, she and the other children again told their names, this time adding something they could do well. "My name is Theresa and I can ride my bike." The third round had them telling about their favorite sections of the local discount store. "My name is Theresa and I like to look at the toys," she announced, her short brown hair bouncing as her confidence grew. During that round, children began to keep track of those who had similar interests. Theresa's friend Peter had been tallying the number of classmates who liked the boa constrictor in the pet department best. "Hey, four people like the snake!" he announced.

The children also celebrated being members of the best class (prettiest, handsomest, smartest, most athletic, best huggers) with music and movement. With the children standing in a circle, I gave directions. "Go to the center and dance when I call out a category that describes you."

I began with lively music and invited all the good helpers to dance first. Theresa and her classmates piled into the center area and began wiggling and giggling to the music. Only one little girl hung back. When I asked her what she did to help her mother, she said, "I fold clothes," then, smiling, she joined the other dancers. Next all the good huggers swayed to a waltz. Before long, the children were calling out more categories: good swimmers, baseball players, cleaner-uppers. I danced along with them, pleased that they were already beginning to know and appreciate each other.

Later, as sunlight streamed in through our wall of southern windows, the children listed topics they'd like to study during the year. Will wanted to explore helicopters and Egyptian mummies because, as he said, "I like ancient times." Katie had brought a children's magazine with an article about bandicoots, so we added this Australian rodent to our list. Peter wanted to study snakes and wolves. Bryan grinned and said, "Baseball! No, I really mean frogs." Emily suggested rainbows, and Theresa nodded her approval. Roger and Rodrick shouted "Indians" in unison after collaborating briefly. Lief thought we should learn about the whole world. That gave me a chance to add my favorite topic, cotton. When our study poster was filled, we selected the first few topics on which the children would begin collecting materials.

Beginning with the rainbow theme, the children wrote a formula poem about the color red. We practiced reading it sitting down, standing up, standing on one foot, with our hands on our hips, with our elbows in the air, in groups of tennis-shoe wearers, boys, girls, brown eyes, blue eyes, and half a dozen other child-thought-of ways. "I can read that by myself!" Bryan and Danielle were among the first to try a solo reading, but before the day was over everyone had read the poem independently. The children traced and illustrated copies to share with their parents.

AUGUST 16

Our circle began with reports on parents' reactions to the red poem. A number of children said, "My mama said, 'Good.'"

Bryan said, "I know my mama was proud because she smiled, and she almost never smiles."

Katie said, "My dad said I was the best reader in the world."

Rodrick said, "My dad gave me a high five," and he demonstrated by slapping his hand into the air.

Charles said, "My mama said, 'Get outta here, boy, I don't have time for that.'"

Theresa said, "I read it to my mom and my dad and my sister and my brother, and my mom put it on the refrigerator."

Later in the morning, we combined words from the poem with names of class members to write sentences: Bryan loves watermelon. Theresa loves red watermelon. Will loves the American flag. Mrs. Swain loves ____. The children wrote their own names in the blank, illustrated each page and stapled their pages so that each owned a personal copy of the first class book. Theresa and Kylie rehearsed reading the book sitting shoulder-to-shoulder.

AUGUST 17

Blue was the topic for the next class poem. The favorite line was "police car light." Every time the children read it, they squealed and giggled. Rather than have the children trace this poem, I conducted a ten-minute mini-lesson, helping them form letters and write the poem on tablet paper. Later they illustrated it and rehearsed reading it in the large group, in pairs, and independently.

Cameras became the focus for the last hour of school today. Sitting in our sharing circle, I explained the National Writing Project teacher research grant that allowed us to purchase six 35mm student cameras, a teacher camera, film, developing, and publishing equipment for our classroom. "I'm writing about you, so I'll be taking photographs of you all year to illustrate my text. I thought you would enjoy having cameras to take photographs of the things you want to write about," I told the children.

Twenty-three pairs of hands reached for the cameras. "I want to; I want to; I want to!" they begged. The next question, "Can we take them home?" I answered with, "After you learn to use them," and watched children scramble into an attentive circle in record time. The cameras went around the circle, each child practicing opening the shutter, taking a photograph, winding the film, and closing the shutter. We made a chart for checking out the cameras. Six children took cameras home this afternoon.

AUGUST 20

What causes a rainbow? I used this question to begin a discussion that netted wonderful explanations. "The clouds," Roger explained. "No, no, it's colors. It's colors going up in the sky," Ethel said. "I think it's the sun shining on water in the air," Peter mused. Theresa smiled and looked from one classmate to another as the unfolding conversation led into a science lesson. Later, after we shared a big book in which a fairy paints a rainbow in the sky, I invited the children to take off their shoes and socks and follow me outside. The parade of barefoot teacher and children must have looked a little strange to passing motorists as it made its way across the grassy campus to the front of the school. There, in a clearing flanked by magnolia trees and pyracantha bushes, we made and played in rainbows, thanks to the janitor's garden hose and bright August sun. Back in the classroom, the children drew pictures, talked in pairs about their illustrations, and went home to tell their parents about rainbows.

AUGUST 21

Green, purple, yellow. "I want to write my own," several children chanted at the conclusion of brainstorming for objects and feelings to represent these colors. A vote settled the matter, and each child wrote an independent color poem, carefully selecting words and phrases from our collaborative "thinking paper." As they wrote, several children asked for words that were not on the paper. I encouraged the children to help me write the words. "What do you hear at the beginning? What do you hear next? What do you hear last?" I usually supplied the vowels, but some children are learning to hear most of the consonants no matter what their position in words.

Theresa's parents met with me today for our first formal conference. Seated on benches in a sunlit alcove filled with green plants, I asked them to tell me about Theresa's reactions to school thus far. They replied with accounts of a child who bounces around the house singing and sharing what she's learning, but then their concern about Theresa's reading surfaced. They knew the strong emphasis that had been placed on

4

phonics in kindergarten was not right for Theresa, yet they really didn't understand how she'd learn to read without it.

I explained my approach to teaching reading, an approach that has evolved as a result of my professional study and careful observation of how children learn. Early in each school day, I read several books to the children, books that I think they might be ready to learn to read. Most of those we read two or three times, with the children joining in on subsequent readings. Sometimes this takes place in a large group with all the children focused on a big book or sharing copies of a book. Sometimes I read in this fashion with small groups of children who have shown interest in particular books. Often we reread favorite books introduced earlier in the year. Discussions following these readings focus first on the stories and the characters. I ask questions like, "Why do you think … ? What if … ? and, Can you retell this story?" Then for a few minutes I ask questions to help children focus on elements of language that appear in the books. "How many times can you find the word *where* on this page?" "What other words in this book begin like *where*?" "How many different characters talked on this page? How can you tell?" The focus for each book depends on the needs of the children at the time and on the language elements that book has to offer.

I explained to Theresa's mother that the children select one book from our large classroom library to "work on." That means the child makes a commitment to learn to read that particular book. (In the case of a very difficult book, we adjust the assignment to learning to read a page or two.) Sometimes everyone works on their books independently as I circulate, giving assistance to those who request it. Most days, children who have chosen the same book gather in small groups and help each other. Two or three times each week the children bring their chosen books to a reading conference with me.

As Theresa tells me about the story she has chosen, I make notes in her literacy folder. Sometimes I record her exact words; sometimes I just note whether she identifies the characters, whether she gives a sequence of details, or tells the main idea of the story. Then I spotlight an area of comprehension for her. I may help her sort out what happened at the beginning, middle, and end of a story. I may help her relate the story to her personal experience. Next, I invite her to read to me, sometimes the whole book, sometimes her favorite pages, sometimes pages I select.

Again I note her behavior, whether she reads with expression or word by word, whether or not she points with her finger as she reads and whether that hinders expression. I note words she miscalls and whether her mistakes appear to be errors related to context, language structure, or phonics. I note the strategies she uses when she encounters an unknown word, whether she stops totally, asks for my help, rereads, or attempts to use a combination of phonics and story content.

Later on we'll begin having reading workshop each morning for an hour or so. For ten to fifteen minutes the children and I will read books of choice. While they may choose to read the books they are working on, children are just as likely to choose books they already read fluently or books they've never heard before, or children's magazines or atlases. Next, all of us, myself included, write in our journals. Throughout the year, I'll be helping them to discover different ways to write about their reading, but they are also free to write about anything that's on their minds.

Then we move back to our sharing circle, where each child has the option of reading the journal entry or passing. It is in the circle where I see the children actually learning from each other. They feel free to interrupt and discuss each other's journal entries. I feel free to call their attention to something new a classmate has learned to do, with the expectation that others will soon follow that lead.

Soon Theresa will be writing collaboratively as well as independently. Because everyone takes part in these writings, the collaborative pieces make wonderful material for whole class reading. Independently, the children will draft books which they'll keep in their writing folders until they have a chance to share them with their friends and with me in writing conferences. They'll learn to revise by adding information, by adding detail, and hopefully by incorporating other writers' techniques they discover as we read. Of course, they'll write different kinds of books — fact based on their photographs, fiction based on imagination, then later fact based on research we'll do in the spring. The phonics will come into play here as Theresa and the other children strive to write so that others can enjoy their work.

I'll also be reading novels to the children, about a chapter a day, beginning with *Squanto, Friend of the Pilgrims* by Clyde Bulla. After lunch each day the children will talk about what has happened in the book and predict what lies in store for the characters. Then they'll role play some of the action as I reread it. Sometimes we'll write about the novel to help the children develop their abilities to remember and understand a sophisticated story line and to provide models for writing about their independent reading.

I gave Theresa's parents a journal article, "Learning to Read in New Zealand," which describes a reading program that closely resembles my approaches. I encouraged Theresa's parents to follow this pattern for helping Theresa read at home: read the book or story *to* Theresa, then read it *with* her several times, then encourage her to read independently.

Theresa's mom volunteered to come twice a week to read with two of Theresa's classmates. After her parents left, I opened the envelope that contained background information about Theresa. I could see that though Theresa had had some physical problems, there was nothing evident in her background that would seriously limit her learning.

Theresa was born April 24, 1984; 6 lbs, 14 oz; 36 weeks gestation. Labor was induced due to my suffering from toxemia. Theresa was born approximately 4 weeks premature but healthy. Theresa suffered frequent ear infections and had tubes placed in both ears at 13 months of age. Even with tubes in place, Theresa still had 5 to 6 ear infections a year. Theresa's walking and talking developed normally. Because I am a teacher, Theresa attended day care.

0-1 year: Home of sitter who had 1 other infant 4 days a week. One day a week she went to Day Care at the hospital where her father worked. It was an excellent center, but because of the cost of having older sister there also, we opted for home care.

1-2 years: Home of a sitter with 2 other children, 1 younger and 1 older thanTheresa, 4 days a week, hospital day care 1 day.

2-3 years: Home of aunt with son the same age as Theresa and an infant 3 days a week. Day care 2 days.

3-31/2 years: Home of aunt 2 days a week. Day care 3 days a week. Theresa was an adaptable, flexible child with an even temper.

7

Before we moved to Mississippi, Theresa's 4-year-old day care class teacher questioned Theresa's readiness for kindergarten the next year since she did not know all of the alphabet and the sounds.

Theresa attended the local academy's kindergarten program at age 5. Difficulty with phonetic sounds showed up by October. We worked at home on letter sounds and blending. We communicated with the teacher to try to keep Theresa's self-esteem up because she was feeling so negative about her abilities. We had a formal hearing evaluation done at a local university in March as requested by the teacher. The teacher was concerned because Theresa would be watching and paying attention but when it came time to do skills, she would not know what was being asked of her.

Test results showed Theresa was hearing within normal limits. Theresa was seen and evaluated at another university's diagnostic clinic in June 1990. Test results showed 'slight hearing loss at given frequencies, and imperfect vision at near point range.' Intelligence tests showed Theresa was 'functioning intellectually in the average range with stronger abilities noted in the verbal area.' It was recommended that we check further into hearing/vision. We met with an ophthalmologist and an ontologist in July. The results showed slight near vision problems, but no treatment was required. There was slight fluid behind the ear drum, but not enough to require treatment at the time. We were told Theresa might distort some sounds. We received the Metropolitan Readiness Test results back from the test that had been taken in the kindergarten classroom in April. Performance Rating was within the 'average' range.

It was recommended that Theresa be retained in kindergarten due to the lack of success in mastering skills in reading necessary to go to their first grade reading program.

We decided that Theresa would find more success in a less phonetic reading program. Her maturity level was satisfactory and had not been an issue in retention recommendations. Theresa knew that we were debating her repeating kindergarten. She had accepted that.

When the decision was made to change schools and go on to first grade, she questioned it slightly but then totally accepted it.

AUGUST 23

I introduced the children to their journals and invited them to draw or write about their favorite school-related activities. The children drew horizontal and vertical lines to create four sections in which to show their ideas. The assistant teacher, student teacher, and I circulated and took dictation from children who requested that we write one of their ideas. Theresa's entry shows her enthusiasm for using the cameras.

AUGUST 27

Theresa completed reading a series of eight emergent readers published by the Wright Group. These tiny paperback books lend themselves to early success in reading the repetitious sentence patterns and clear, colorful illustrations. Theresa's mother called last night, excited about

Theresa's progress. She said that these books were instrumental in helping Theresa realize that she could read.

AUGUST 28

Sitting in her table grouping — six student desks joined together — Theresa chose a big book, *Harbors,* by Donald Crews to read today. The book is filled with terms for each kind of ship found in a city harbor, many that I doubt Theresa has heard of. Sometimes when children choose a totally unfamiliar book, I hear them making up text they think might go along with the illustrations. Last year I overheard Laura as she "read" an old fairy tale book. "It all happened a very long time ago," she said, "probably about 1789 ... " Theresa was silent, absorbing herself in the illustrations, turning the pages slowly as she rested her head in her open palm.

After lunch, I invited the children to think about their own thinking by lying on the floor in a fashion similar to that depicted by a bulletin board picture showing a boy lying under an apple tree. Above the boy a caption reads, "What is he thinking?" The children brainstormed the various things that the boy might be thinking. "He's thinking that apple is going to fall on him." "He's thinking about playing baseball." "He's thinking about going to visit his dad." Then they reclined on the floor with the assignment to let their thoughts wander and, at the same time, to notice the topics of their thoughts. Soft music played as the children closed their eyes in this first experience of thinking about their own thinking.

They made the second entry in their journals following this activity. I asked them to write and/or draw to explain their thoughts. As I often do at the beginning of the school year, I assisted with spelling when they asked for help. Journals sometimes pose a threat to children who want to write but who don't yet feel comfortable even with invented spelling. My assistance is often in the form of individual mini-lessons to help them realize how sometimes they might use inventions instead of conventional spelling. After about three weeks, we begin daily journaling in the reading workshop and I am no longer available to assist with spelling during this time because, as I explain, I am writing in my own journal.

Note from Theresa's mother:

End of August
Bringing home a book about circus animals Her reading is choppy
and she needs some help but she makes progress every time she reads
it. By end of a 2 week period, she has totally impressed herself (and
Us!) with her abilities and is excited about reading!

Chew it. Blow it. Pop it.
Stretch it 'til it's long.
Pull it. Smack it.
Wind it all between your toes.

SEPTEMBER 4

"Please read *Jesse Bear, What Will You Wear?*" Roger begged. "It has a red shirt in it. It goes with our red poem." He had discovered the book during reading workshop and had shared it with several friends. So today we read and reread this book, the children joining in the reading as they became more and more familiar with the text. The two classroom copies are suddenly in great demand during independent reading times. This afternoon, Roger and Rodrick lay flat on their backs with copies of the book held high above their heads. I overheard them reading it together as they waited for the last bus, "Sleep in my eyes, and stars in the skies, moon on my bed, and dreams in my head."

SEPTEMBER 5

"Jesse Bear, what will you wear? What will you wear in the morning? My shirt of red pulled over my head, over my head in the morning," read the girls, then the boys, then those wearing red shirts, then those wearing yellow shirts, and so on until all had read and giggled and beamed with pride. On another day, I might have written a few lines from the book on the chalkboard or on chart paper so the entire class could see to read together. But all that preparation isn't always necessary. The large print in this book allowed everyone to see as I pointed to the text, and, as small children often do, they cuddled up close to my chair while I read.

Theresa selected a page showing Jesse Bear wearing rice in his hair as her favorite; so did three other children. Lief and Danielle, two of our five red-heads, chose the page where Jesse Bear's pants are covered with ants. Bryan liked the page where Jesse Bear's hand is covered with sand. Emily liked the floral borders around all the pages. Roger and Rodrick chose the last page, the one they'd read together yesterday.

Gathering into a circle, we asked each other, "____Bear, what will you wear?" One by one the children answered, "I will wear my red shirt or blue pants or army suit." Orlicia said she'd wear a rose between her toes. Rodrick said he'd wear the moon on his bed. Several children named an item of clothing: dress, socks, shorts. On the second and third rounds of the circle, I encouraged everyone to add words to describe the clothes: blue dress, rainbow socks, bluejean shorts.

SEPTEMBER 6

I gave each child a paper with his or her name typed at the beginning of the "___ Bear, what will you wear?" question at the top of the page. A large area for drawing separated the question sentence from two lined writing spaces at the bottom. The children talked as they drew pictures of themselves dressed in their favorite clothes. After sharing the drawings with partners, they wrote their responses in the writing spaces at the bottom of the page. The beginning of the sentence, "I will wear my ..." was written on the chalkboard for reference. The assistant teacher, Betty Nail, and I circulated as the children drew their pictures and helped them spell the words to describe their clothes.

Theresa colored intently with a pink crayon, pink tongue sticking out of a corner of her mouth "Do you need help spelling any words for your page?" I asked.

"Yes, I'm going to write 'I will wear my pink dress.'"

"Do you need me to write the whole sentence for you?" I asked. I had just worked with two children who could not yet copy from the board.

"No," Theresa said, pointing to the chalkboard, "I can look up there for part."

"What do you need my help with?"

"Pink dress," she smiled.

I pulled a pad of stickie notes out of my pocket and laid it on her desk, "I'll write on a stickie note and you can put it in your writing folder in case you ever need these words again. Now let's start with *pink*. Say *pink* and tell me the first sound you hear."

"Pink, pink, p," she grinned. I wrote a p.

"Now, say it again and listen for the very last sound."

"Pink, pink, g?" she asked. I nodded. "Pink, k?" he asked.

"Yes, wow! You have really good ears to hear the last sound. Now I'm going to show you something." I wrote the *i* and drew a short line where the *nk* was to go. "Listen to me say pink." I said the word a few times, exaggerating the sound of *nk*. Then I had Theresa say it in the same fashion while feeling the vibrations in her larynx. "When you hear that funny sound at the end of a word, it's going to be spelled *nk*, so I'm going to write *nk*, and that's how you spell *pink*."

Using a similar technique, Theresa and I spelled dress. Like many children, /dr/ sounded like /gr/ to her. However, she heard and identified the /s/ sound right away. I wrote the word on the stickie note, and as I walked away, I noticed the pink crayon and pink tongue once again happily at work.

Sᴇᴘᴛᴇᴍʙᴇʀ 7

I typed the children's written responses to the "What will you wear" question, adding quotation marks and "said ___ Bear." Then I taped their drawings onto the newly typed pages and made six copies of each. At a "book party," Theresa and her classmates traded five of their pages with each other to create personal versions of a book called *Room 9 Bears, What*

Will You Wear? Mrs. Nail and I circulated with staplers while children shuffled their pages, arranging them in the order that seemed best.

Gathering on the rug for a class reading, we practiced each child's page together. "Everybody who has Danielle's page, turn to it and help us read," I'd say until we had read all the pages. Then the children practiced reading their individual books, consulting friends when they needed help.

Coloring the copies of the illustrations required more consultation. Children grouped and regrouped themselves on the rug, three or four of them coloring one friend's page before moving to another page and another group.

After lunch, the children copied their own sentences, complete with quotation marks, onto strips of poster paper and glittered the quotation marks. We practiced reading the strips, first reading whole sentences, then reading "just the words that came out of Bryan's or Peter's mouth." Reflecting back to the sharing circle where they had told what they'd wear, we separated the actual spoken words from the explanatory words, the words that tell who is talking. The glittered quotation marks became the "lips" surrounding the actual spoken words. Later, I assisted the children as they searched favorite books for sentences containing direct quotations and copied those on tablet paper, highlighting the quotation marks with markers.

Note from Theresa's mother:

> *Sept. 8-9*
> *On a couple of occasions over the weekend, out of the blue, she offered to spell a couple of words on her own that had been mentioned in the conversation. One I remember was STAND. The spelling attempt was initiated by her. (spelled it correctly on her own) This is the first time that I remember her really initiate the spelling of words on her own.*

SEPTEMBER 10

Sometimes learning experiences grow out of pure fun. I had encouraged the children's mothers to send snacks for the class. As I watched their delight over cookies, it occurred to me that they would have a marvelous time chewing, talking about, and writing about bubble gum. So last week, the children brainstormed all the things they could do with gum: chew it, pop it, blow it, stretch it, pull it, stick it on your nose, wind it between your toes. Next, I passed out bubble gum, and photographed them as they unwrapped, chewed, blew, popped, stretched, and otherwise played with their gum.

Today, the children collaborated to combine their brainstormed ideas and their gum-chewing photographs into a *Big Gum Book*. Carefully, they matched each of their photos with the sentence that best described it. Since there was no photograph to go with their favorite sentence, "Wind it all between your toes," they decided to illustrate it with a photo of Bryan laughing because, "It shows that we think it's funny." I also made individual copies, minus photographs, which each child illustrated and practiced reading with partners.

Theresa chose a preprimer as her next reading project, and I modeled by reading stories to her. Emily and Ethel joined us on the rug and then stayed to hear Theresa read. She self-corrected the sentence, "Up went the little bug" which she first read as, "Hop went the little bug." I noticed that the miscue was consistent with the context and that she made use of phonetic knowledge in making the correction. After she finished reading, I asked her how she knew the word was *up* and not *hop*. "I just knew," she replied. It feels good to see her confidence grow, but knowing how she knows is important, too. In time, I hope she'll be able to describe her ways of knowing for herself and for me.

Note from Theresa's mother:

> *Sept. 10 Brought new book home to practice reading from. Jumped right into it even the 1st night!*

SEPTEMBER 11

Peter is very happy now that we've begun studying wolves. He brought a magazine article in which photographs of wolves illustrate their behavior. Because of our camera project, the children's interest focused not only on wolves, but also on photography as craft. "How did he (the author) get so close?" "Look at those little ones rolling around." "It looks like he took this one from up in the sky. How?"

I decided to capitalize on their interest. Turning the pages slowly, I asked children to describe what the wolves were doing in each photograph. Then I asked, "Did the author arrange the wolves in a row with all of them looking straight into the camera?"

"No, no," the children giggled. "He just took the picture."

"Which would be more interesting," I pressed, "wolves in a row or wolves behaving naturally?"

"Naturally, just doing their thing," Peter offered.

"What can we learn about taking photographs from this wolf article?" I asked.

"Uh, oh," Bryan groaned. "I shouldn't have made my family all sit on the sofa for a picture." Several other children groaned with him. I reassured them that posed photographs have a place, but that everyone would have many chances to take candid shots.

Peter grinned throughout this discussion. Finally he blurted out, "It was going to be a surprise, but I got a hummingbird through the window. It was flying!" Because of the camera project all of us are becoming aware of the many uses of photography as illustration. I had hoped the NWP grant would help us to write like readers and read like writers. It is also changing us as "readers" of photography.

Our study of wolves inspired the class to compose this story collaboratively:

> *The black wolf went up the hill.*
> *The black wolf met a white wolf.*
> *The wolves said, "Good morning."*

After reading it all together, standing, sitting, and in groups of boys and girls, several pairs of children role-played the story. Naturally, the "actors" faced each other in their enactments of two wolves meeting. I changed the word *met* to *ran after*. One child then turned away as the other chased her. I asked several children to explain why changing the words made the actors change directions. Danielle explained, "Well, if they met, they have to look at each other, but if one ran after the other one, he has to be behind."

We took another cycle through the concept of direct quotations. "Let's read the last sentence and count the words in it," I said. Then, to emphasize the words within the quotation marks, "Now just read the words that came out of the wolves' mouths. How many?"

The follow-up assignment was to copy and illustrate the story. When Theresa came for her conference, I noticed that her picture showed two wolves standing on a horizontal line at the bottom of the page. I asked her to read the story again and tell me where the wolves should be. "On a hill," she said. I suggested that she tape another piece of paper to the bottom of her picture so that she could add a hill under her wolves. She bounced back to her seat and said to Danielle, "I have to throw this away and start over." Amazed and dismayed at her readiness to discard her work, I called her back and asked her to bring her paper and a clean page with her. When the new page was placed under the original picture, she saw a way to revise. Having a roll of tape in her desk added to her independence in completing the revision.

She was so willing to toss her picture ... I want her to understand revision as a normal part of any composing process. I don't want her to trash her work and start from ground zero. Just as I have accepted her where she is developmentally, I want her to recognize her own strengths and her capacity to build on them.

SEPTEMBER 12

Before reading a chosen book to me, Theresa announced that her book was easy. She answered questions about the illustrations and the problem in the story she read. She pointed to words with her finger, but read with some expression. When confronted with the word "hid," she asked, "What's that word?" without first trying other strategies. Later today Theresa helped Tanya understand the math concept of "one more." The girls added one block at a time to a stack and wrote the corresponding numerals on a small poster.

Note from Theresa's mother:

> *Sept. 12 Read to two neighbor ladies. Excited about it and willing to do it. Did a great job!*

SEPTEMBER 13

Note from Theresa's mother:

> *Sept. 13 Wanted to write words! I asked her what she wanted to write. She didn't care ... just wanted to write words! I wrote some*

down. She said, 'No, not that! WORDS.' (She meant sentences.) So we wrote down a couple of sentences and she copied them. I showed her the difference between words and sentences. She then got the dictionary down and copied words of her choice and then asked what she had spelled.

We've been in school less than a month and already I'm seeing so much progress in Theresa. She's happy. She selects her own books. She isn't afraid to ask for help when she needs it. She seems to know the kind of help she needs. I'm anxious to see her learn some self-help strategies, especially in reading. The notes from her mother are giving me a picture of how Theresa takes her school knowledge into the home setting. They also show a pretty terrific, wonderfully supportive mother! I'm wishing that I had this same kind of information swap going on with all the children's parents. Occasional conferences just aren't enough.

SEPTEMBER 14

As class members composed number stories about wolves, I wrote them on the chalkboard. Eventually, we revised one story into a collaborative number story. In the process, Theresa's story was erased. After I made the assignment to copy and solve the class problem, Theresa said, "I want to do my own, but you erased it." I rewrote it for her to copy and solve. (Her story is at the top of the next page.) Following her lead, two other children opted to write individual stories.

Note from Theresa's mother:

Sept. 14 Brought home a math story problem that she had made up and written. It was so beautiful, it brought tears to my eyes!

Theresa chose to read the collaboratively-written *Our Big Gum Book* to me. Emily and Ethel joined her as she read, all three engaging in conversation about their classmates' photographs on each page. "Pick the kind you want." They read. "Chew it. Blow it. Pop it. Stretch it 'til it's long. Pull it. Smack it. Wind it all between your toes."

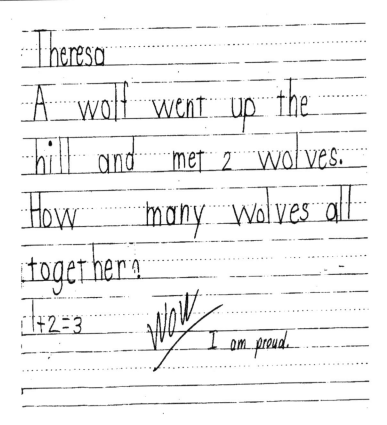

Theresa

A wolf went up the hill and met 2 wolves. How many wolves all together?

1+2=3   Wow   I am proud.

SEPTEMBER 15

When I asked Theresa where she preferred to read, at home or at school, she replied, "Both." Then, as she read, she pointed with her finger on most, but not all, of the pages. "I've been practicing," she announced proudly.

I've noticed that some children, those who don't yet recognize the correlation between written and spoken word units, need to point to individual words until they recognize that relationship. Theresa is not one of those children; she understands that one cluster of letters will equal one spoken word. It seems to me that once children internalize that concept, finger-pointing slows their reading and impedes fluency. Sometimes I ask children like Theresa why they are pointing. Some will say,

"To keep my place." Others will say, "I don't know." Theresa is in the latter category. Today her reading was word by word whether or not she used her finger as a pointer. With Theresa's history of being asked to blend sounds into words, I'm wondering if her definition of reading is more closely tied to pronouncing words than to meaning.

A few days ago, she found an obsolete basal shelved with our library books. "This is a reading book!" she announced. Her comment still haunts me. If a "reading" book looks like a basal, what are all the beautiful trade books for? Next week, we'll begin having reading workshop every day. Maybe seeing the other children reading all sorts of books will free her to read a variety of children's literatire.

Theresa is becoming aware of strategies for writing using sources for references. When I asked her to name her favorite book, she said, '*Sun Up*" and explained why. "I know how to write *turtle*. I can just look in here. Now I'll know how to write it in my wolf story. It's on the board and it's in my book."

SEPTEMBER 17

This was the first day of formal reading workshop, the real heart of my reading program, the application component that is supported by shared reading, writing, teacher modeling, and spotlight lessons. For ten to fifteen minutes everyone reads, then we discuss briefly one or two of the many ways we might react to our reading. Journal writing is the second phase of the workshop, and again for ten to fifteen minutes everyone writes in reaction to their reading or about anything else that reflects their thinking at the moment. Then we gather in a sharing circle to read the entries aloud.

Each year I begin reading workshop earlier. The first year it was the first week of December; the second year, the first week of November; then the first of October. Now here I am beginning in the middle of

September. I think these children have had enough experience reading and reflecting with the whole class and in small groups so that they can do independent reading and reflecting. I hope they are ready for it. And I think it's time for them to see Mrs. Nail and me read and write as adults.

I explained that I'd set the timer for ten minutes. They were to gather two or three books they'd like to read and prepare to read at their desks without interrupting the reading of their friends or me. Similar instructions prefaced the journal writing time. In a mini-lesson, I showed them how to write the date numerically. In a brief open discussion, several children told what they'd read and what they planned to write about in their journals. Then I set the timer for ten minutes and we all wrote. This time, I was not available to spell or encourage or answer questions. I was writing too, and I was not to be disturbed.

Theresa perused *What's It Like to be a Teacher?* today and copied the title into her journal.

SEPTEMBER 18

The first photographs taken by the children came back today. Peter's hummingbird photo turned out nicely. Darren had taken a shot of his brother digging around in his closet. "What's he looking for?" Roger asked. Katie had candid shots of her mother in the dentist's chair. The class giggled and began to tell their own dentist stories. Danielle's photos included one of her sister playing the piano. "What song is she playing?" everyone wanted to know. Several children had carefully posed their families; those photos received little attention from the group. Someone had taken a snapshot of a television; blurred streaks crossed the screen. I'm glad I didn't tell them in advance what kind of photographs to take. They're discovering for themselves!

During our prewriting conference focusing on the photograph she chose to write about, Theresa said, "I took a picture of my friends, Meghan and Hilary."

"What else?" I asked.

"Ducks. I took a picture of ducks, too."

Theresa took the photograph to her desk and began to write. A short time later, she tugged on my sleeve. "How do you spell Meghan? Will you write it on a piece of paper?" Theresa had already written a capital *M* on her paper. She was not only aware of the beginning sound, but she was willing to risk writing it. By asking me to write the word on a piece of paper, she was also showing that she understood where she was developmentally, that she needed to copy the printed word, that she didn't think she could remember how to write the word if I spelled orally for her. Shortly she was back asking the same question about the name Hilary, which she knew began with *H*.

The invented spellings on Theresa's completed writing showed some knowledge of initial consonants and word length. I noted also that she used consistent spelling — *piev*, for example, for the word *picture*.

I took a picture
of my friends, Meghan and
Hilary.
I took a picture of
ducks, too.

I invited Theresa, along with other children, to the rug to read with me. Several minutes later, Theresa still hadn't come to the rug. "I can't find my book," she said perched on her chair, her chin resting in her palm.

"Have you looked for it?" I asked.

"I looked and it's not in there," she replied.

"You must take everything out of your desk until you find it," I told her. I heard papers rattle and saw the top of her head bob up and down as she knelt to the floor to search the cavity of her desk. Finally, she joined us on the rug, opening her book as she settled into the circle of readers.

Several afternoons, Theresa and her mother have reappeared in the classroom after dismissal. Theresa, it seems, does not take responsibility for taking books and papers home. Together, she and her mother go through her desk to find the needed items. Is Theresa simply forgetting, or does she fail to accept responsibility for the tools of a learner? Does she view her mother and me as responsible for her learning?

SEPTEMBER 19

How did I ever teach without reading workshop? The private reading and reflection time for tying professional reading to written reflections about my children helps me understand their development and make decisions about my teaching. Starting the workshop is like coming home after a long trip. Yet, a stranger walking in during our workshop might accuse us of wasting time. The children are still learning to settle in during the reading phase ... and it certainly isn't silent reading! Last year a colleague walked in during our reading time and was taken aback when I motioned for her to be quiet. "Listen to all the noise they're making," she protested. True, but engagement when you're six or seven years old doesn't necessarily mean silence. From the first day, Peter, Katie, Orlicia, and Kylie sank into their books, emerging reluctantly after the timer sounded. Engagement will happen for all the children. It takes time and faith. I have the faith; I'll give them the time.

Roger is still struggling with a little book that has only two words per page, but for the first time yesterday he asked for help by spelling *look* to me. He's been stopping on every few words and sitting in silence without using any kind of strategy to keep going. It's good to see him asking for help. His friend Ivan is once again reading *This Little Piggy*, a Wright Group emergent reader. Yesterday after he read it to me, he strutted across the room bragging, "I read that book!"

While other children were putting away their sweaters this morning, Danielle announced, "I want to read this rhyme." Later, reading "The Three Bears," she suddenly hiccoughed. We both giggled; she must be the guilty one, I said — she ate the porridge and hiccoughed.

"Little Red Locks," I said, "Wouldn't that be a good book."

"Can I make one?" she asked. "Can I copy part of this? Will you help me spell? Can I stay in and work on it at recess?" She skipped off with a supply of paper and inspiration.

Kylie is referring to the "Growl Your Name" wall poster as she writes in her journal. Peter is drawing. He's filled a page with carefully detailed Ninja Turtles, but he fulfilled the requirement to have words on the page by writing, "I lake (like)." at the top.

Near the end of the reading phase this morning I noticed that Theresa wasn't reading. She had turned sideways in her chair and was casting a forlorn look in my direction. The saddest return look I could muster did not persuade her to reopen her book. Now, during journal writing time, I see that she is writing with a fat hot pink pencil. I can see two lines of print broken into word units.

I can ride my bike in the street.

I had a short conference with Theresa's mom today after she finished reading with Roger and Tanya. I shared my observations about Theresa's preference for old basals and my goal to broaden her reading to include good children's literature. I suggested that her fluency and understanding of sophisticated sentence structure would develop more rapidly if she were reading a wider variety of books. We decided not to press the issue yet because Theresa is enjoying reading for the first time and needs to gain a little more confidence first. Then her mother asked a perfectly obvious question that I hadn't thought to clarify for her, "Why does Theresa sometimes write neatly and with good spelling and sometimes not?" As examples, we compared Theresa's number story about wolves with her journal entries and her story about Meghan, Hilary, and the ducks.

"I try to achieve a balance between teacher-transcribed stories which children copy and independent writing where children take a risk using invented spelling," I explained. Several times each week the children copy stories they've written collaboratively or independently. I take dictation from them and write their stories correctly either on chart paper, for the entire class, or on tablet paper, for individual children. (There are always one or two children who cannot copy from one page to another. I write directly on their papers with a thin yellow highlighter. They trace over my writing, and the highlighter is almost covered. Their completed work looks like everyone else's.) Daily, though, the children write independently, using whatever knowledge they've internalized about the shapes of letters, sentence structure, spelling, and mechanics. Struggling to write independently heightens children's awareness of correct forms when they encounter them in work to be copied or in books. Studying their attempts at independent writing is also the most valuable diagnostic tool I have for assessing their strengths and needs as writers. Theresa copied my transcription of the number story; she wrote the story about her friends and the ducks independently.

When I returned from the parent conference, the children giggled and pointed to the chalkboard where Mrs. Nail was transcribing a conversation that took place in my absence. Danielle and Katie clamored to read it aloud first. Eventually, though, all the children paired up to read and laugh.

"Where is Mrs. Swain?" Danielle asked.

"She's in the land of no return!" said Katie.

SEPTEMBER 20

Theresa came in at 10:30 today. (Her mother told me that she's worried about Theresa not feeling well and is thinking about having her tested. I inquired whether Theresa's stomach ache might be school-related. Her mother assured me that it is not, that Theresa is enjoying school.)

I introduced the children to one of many procedures we use to celebrate ourselves and learn about each other — a conversation party. Each child divided a piece of paper into four sections. In section one, they illustrated and wrote about something they can do well. In section two, something they haven't yet learned to do. In section three, someone who makes them happy. (As the children wrote the names of friends and family members in section three, Katie reminded everyone to use a capital letter at the beginning of the names.) In section four, they shared something they worry about. Theresa's page is shown below.

The sentence in section one is similar to her September 19 journal entry, "I ride my bike." Section two reads, "I can't jump rope." Section three names her sister, Mackenzie, as the person who makes her happy. Section four indicates that Theresa worries about bears.

I asked Danielle to help model what we'd do at the conversation party. Standing before the class, she and I asked questions based on the writings and drawings we saw on each other's papers. Danielle noticed the singer I had drawn in section two. "I wish I could sing," I said, "but it's really hard for me. I have to practice and practice on any song I want to learn."

I asked her about the two people she had drawn in section three. "This one is my big, big sister," she said, "and this one is my next big sister. She's in the third grade. She helps me play the piano."

I passed out pieces of masking tape for taping papers to clothing, set the timer for ten minutes and challenged the children to meet and talk with as many classmates as they could before the bell sounded. "Ask questions to help you learn something new about your friends," I said. "Afterward we'll talk about what we've learned."

During the conversation party, I asked Theresa what kind of bears she worries about. She grinned and said, "Teddy bears." Theresa is obviously a very secure little girl; several children expressed worries about death, nightmares, strangers, and family finances.

Just before lunch, I noticed that Theresa was not working. I reminded her that she needed to finish. Five minutes later, she was still sitting. Another reminder netted the same results. Finally, I asked if she were feeling well. She replied, "I can't find my crayons."

"Take everything out of your desk," I said. "Finding your crayons is your job."

"Okay." She popped down, dug around, found the crayons, spilled them, gathered them up again, and completed her work.

This afternoon, she and her mother returned in search of books and papers that Theresa should have packed in her backpack. As they approached Theresa's desk, I called the mother aside and told her the story of the crayons, leaving Theresa alone to locate the missing materials. Together we worked out a strategy for helping Theresa accept responsibility for her things. Her mother would clarify her expectation that Theresa would keep up with her school materials. I'd make it a point to ask her if she had her things before she left the room. If Theresa was to accept personal responsibility for learning to read and write, she'd first have to accept responsibility for the tools of learning.

Notes from Theresa's mother:

Sept. 23 Wanted to know why one word started with a capital letter and another didn't. (Had just studied it in school.)
Sept. 24 Read again to a neighbor lady. Very comfortable reading orally. Confident. Is correcting herself on words like went and was.

SEPTEMBER 25

Jump over on your left foot.
Jump over to the right.
Jump down on two feet.
Jump, jump, jump.

In celebration of Jereme this morning, we made up a dance to the tune of the Bunny Hop. We called it the Jereme Jump. Around and around the room we bounced, learning about left and right. Most children copied the words to our dance to share with their families. Our early morning celebrations of one child per day let us focus on skills like left and right in a meaningful way. If I were a new teacher, I'd probably need a checklist to insure that we "covered" all the skills. Experience has taught me to trust that the skills can and will be "uncovered" in a myriad of meaningful contexts. I just have to recognize the opportunities to spotlight them.

In addition to a numerical notation for the date, now we're writing the time and sky conditions as part of our journal header each morning. Some children already know how to tell time. As we figure it out together each morning, others will catch on, at their own pace, in their own time. Each morning a child writes the date and time on the board and determines the sky conditions. As we change sun to sunny, cloud to cloudy, rain to rainy, the children are learning that y at the end of some words makes the sound of e.

During journaling time, Theresa again wrote with her fat hot pink pencil. She erased three times in the span of as many minutes. A book lay open on her desk as she wrote, and I wondered whether she was copying or composing. My question was answered when she read this entry in the sharing circle. She'd copied from *Sun Up*.

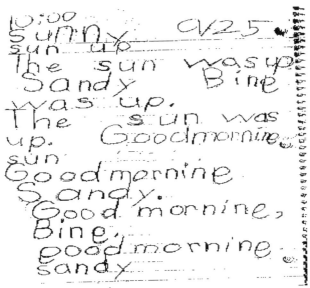

31

Theresa was still finishing math from the day before when I invited her and several other children to read with me on the rug. Without consulting me, she finished her math before joining us. Later I complimented her for taking responsibility for completing her work and for knowing how to join the group quietly.

Note from Theresa's mother:

> *Sept. 25 Asked to read from old kindergarten book that was so hard for her before. Needs help, but proud of herself.*

SEPTEMBER 26

Theresa used a thin blue pencil and erased frequently as she wrote in her journal. She used the yellow eraser to point as she reread her text. In the sharing circle she read, "I went with my mom." Later I asked why she had erased part of her entry. She replied, "I forgot. I didn't want that part." Recently I've had occasion to reread some of my classroom journals from the past few years. It seems that I frequently make note of children's first tendencies to reread as they write. I believe this activity indicates a real engagement with their writing, that they are rereading to verify that the writing reflects their intended meaning. I believe Theresa's rereading as she writes shows that she is writing for a purpose and that she realizes there is structure to our written language.

Note from Theresa's mother:

> *Sept. 26 There was a bee in our car. She spelled it. I asked her how she knew it had two e's. She said, 'I just knew!' She read to a different neighbor. Impressed her with fluid reading and self-correcting.*

SEPTEMBER 27

I tried a new workshop strategy as a result of Charles's response to a question. When asked what he'd been reading about, he grinned and said, "Elizabeth Hen," as he held up the big book of *Elizabeth Hen* by Siobhan Dodds. I realized that some children don't understand what it means to tell what they read *about* as opposed to telling the title of *what* they read. To emphasize the content of their reading, I had the children mentally rehearse what they might say about their reading, then put their books away and talk to a partner for one minute about the reading.

Instructions to the listening partner included asking questions in the event the talking partner stopped talking. We reversed the procedure so that each child experienced talking about a book and supporting a partner's book talk. After the partner activity, the children entered the writing phase of the workshop. I began to watch for any evidence that this added activity would impact the way the children wrote about their reading.

While Theresa's entry did not reflect reactions to reading, it thrilled me because it was her first attempt to truly explain her thinking. In it, she clearly broke the print for word units, used consistent invented spellings, and displayed knowledge of consonants, vowels, and some standard spellings. I shared it with her parents in our conference this afternoon.

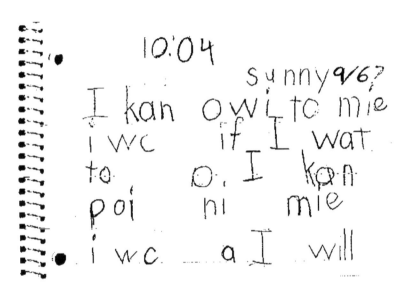

I can go to my house if I want to and I can play in my house and I will

Note from Theresa's mother:

Sept. 27 Had conference today with teacher. At dinner, we asked Theresa what she had done at school today. Her response, 'Too much

to explain. But I wrote in my journal.' She then told us that she wrote ... And I will was the last sentence. I had noticed at the conference that will was spelled correctly. I asked her how she knew how to spell it. She explained, 'One of the boys in the class is named Will.' Hanging on the wall was a 'Gift Poster' for Will and she had looked up there to see how it was spelled.

SEPTEMBER 28

After the reading phase of the workshop, the children shared with partners again before beginning their writing. As they moved into the writing phase, I suggested that they write the same things they had told their partners. Theresa said, "I can't. I couldn't read my book."

"Can you write about the pictures?" I asked.

"I can write what's on my mind." she replied.

Note from Theresa's mother:

Sept. 30 Theresa had the camera home and was talking about how they had six cameras to begin with but now only have five to use. She then said, 'I can spell six, SIX.' I asked if they had been practicing that at school, and she said, 'No, I just can spell it. I can spell seven too.' With seven she went, 'Seven, S, Seeeven E, Sevvven, V, Seveeen, E Sevennn, N, ' but then she said it once more and put an L on the end of it. I asked her to say the word she was spelling again. She said, 'Seven.' I asked her what the ending sound was. She said the word again and answered, 'N! Oh, there is no L just S-E-V-E-N!'

OCTOBER 1

Our student teacher, Jennifer Tutor, is concerned when she sees some children stacking their books, rubbing their hands over the covers, and looking at pictures rather than reading during workshop time. I see a variety of ways to engage with books. Just the holding and stacking and having a desk full adds to the experience. I, too, like to feel the cover of a new book, to place it just so on the shelf, to inspect the jacket and the hard cover. People who love books love more than the print.

During journal time, I asked the children to write with their books closed. Will complained that he needed to write about helicopters, and that he didn't know how. I see that he's opened his book. He's smelling, rolling, poking his pencil. Now, finally, he's putting point to paper. The timer sounds an end to journal writing time; he panics. "I have a lot more to write!" Ten minutes is not long enough to get him going. He needs more cooking time.

Theresa passed rather than read this journal entry to the class this morning. Looking through her journal, I stopped and chuckled. To write this, she copied from an old preprimer and injected her own knowledge of humor. Under the horizontal line, she wrote:

> *Sun Up*
> *The sun was 5 up.*
> *Sandy was 6 up.*
> *Bing was 7 up.*

Later, reading a chosen book to me, Theresa read from a story that had been shared with the class. She misread and did not correct "Ted said," which she read as "the said." (After she finished, I told her there was one part of the story I didn't understand. When I asked her to reread that part, she read it correctly.) She used her finger as a pointer; however, she used appropriate intonation for questions and narrative. She asked for help on the words *it* and *said*. As I sometimes do when children ask for help in the midst of reading, I suggested that she quickly spell the word to me. (Since the children are seated in a circle with me, I am not looking directly at the page and can honestly say that I can't see the word they need.) In this way, their reading is minimally interrupted and I can make a quick diagnosis as to whether they are identifying the letters correctly.

In an attempt to involve her in reading more trade books, I had suggested that she take *Brown Bear, What Do You See?* home yesterday. She appeared at my desk this morning saying, "I need a book."

"Don't you like Brown Bear?"

"Yes," she said, "but I can read it in one night."

"Then you can get another one," I answered, indicating our shelves of colorful paperback books.

"But I want one off that shelf," she said, pointing to the collection of old basals at the back of the room. "I want one with lots of stories in it."

Will had wandered over during this exchange. "When are we gonna start studying cowboys and Indians?" he said, "I've got a lot of books about Indians."

OCTOBER 2

Danielle has a scraped knee this morning. Ethel's wearing new shoes. This is Emily's "day" and she's digging through the poster paper, choosing the color of her compliment quilt. Peter is reading a cartoon story. Charles is intent on copying poems into his journal. I guess having something real to put in his journal might make him feel more comfortable. Friday, Bryan wrote to describe his reading process … how the hard and easy books contribute to his learning. With every passing day, these children become more unique, more diverse, more special.

This morning, with the children gathered on the rug, I read and reread a story, pointing to the text as I said the words. Anchored in place by a freckled hand on my knee, Will interrupted the second reading to ask about a possessive form, "How come it's got a commer?" We stopped and discussed Will's "commer" which, in reality, was an apostrophe. The character in the story owned a pile of junk, and I wanted to help the children understand her.

"Who's seen good stuff on the roadside or at a flea market?" I asked.

Rodrick was hooked, "And your mama said 'come on' and you be wanting to get it!"

As we moved from the teacher-modeled reading into reading workshop, Theresa asked for *I Went Walking* by Sue Williams. After the reading phase I asked for volunteers to tell about a good book. Theresa raised her hand. When I called on her, she paused for thirty to forty seconds before responding, "A whole bunch of animals were following him." I noticed the amount of wait time she seemed to need to gather her thoughts. Theresa had synthesized the details given in the book and produced an original statement to explain the main idea. What might she have said if I had rushed her response? In this journal entry, composed without access to a book, Theresa followed the journaling guidelines I set for the class: react to your reading; then draw a horizontal line and, under it, write whatever is on your mind.

> *I went walking.*
> *What did you see?*
> *I saw a whole bunch of animals.*
>
> ———————————
>
> *Oh, I am going out of town today.*

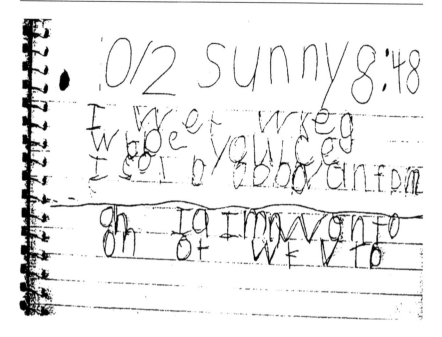

We formed peer learning groups today. I determined that there would be seven groups, and mentally identified the seven children who needed the most support in their learning processes. I had all the children reflect on others who helped them learn. "Think about all the partners you've worked with," I advised, "write the names of two or three people with whom you work best." I made special note of those named by the seven classmates in need of support. Two of those children, Tanya and Charles, named Theresa. To form the groups, my only criterion is that every child be in a group where he or she can both give and receive support. I placed Theresa, Tanya, and Bryan in one group, and they named themselves the Tornados. Theresa explained, "I thought of it. That was my soccer team."

Note from Theresa's mother:

Oct. 2 Brought home a new book. It was difficult for her to read the first night. There were a lot of new words, but she tried hard and didn't get discouraged.

Theresa's little brother, Peter, surely is enjoying Theresa's reading. He likes to listen to her read and when she's done with the book, he tries to read. He really liked Buffy and Mack and still walks around with a book saying, 'Mack up, up Mack.'

OCTOBER 3

People often ask if my students are aware of how our classroom differs from traditional classrooms where children work in workbooks most of the day and read in groups determined by ability. Of course they aren't; as first graders, this is the only classroom they've known. But this morning, as we were walking in the hallway, I overheard a conversation between two boys who were in traditional first grades last year and who are repeating first grade in Room 9.

"I like school now."

"Me too. I used to not like school but now I do."

At the beginning of journaling time Will said, "Ten o' clock! That doesn't give us much time to write." I commented on his need for lots of writing time. As he nodded agreement, Rodrick said, "Me too!" A visitor opened the classroom door during journaling time. My thoughts evaporated, and I wondered if the children had the same experience. I looked around the room; Katie and Chris were rereading their entries; Theresa was numbering eleven thoughts under the horizontal line. (First graders often quantify their writing.) "I love you mom and dad" is number 10.

October 4

This morning Theresa had several sheets of paper on her desk and smiled as she wrote with a 3-colored ball point pen. Switching to a pencil, she wrote and erased with her arm and head resting on her desk. She glanced at me once or twice and, sweeping eraser crumbs away, turned back to her journal, bright red fingernails flashing as she wrote, erased, swept, and wrote again.

I love you Mom and Dad
Mackenzie and Peter
I like Meghan and Hilary, too.

Yesterday in the circle, Danielle read a question from her journal and received responses from the class. I asked Danielle to reread her entry several times, asking questions that helped the children discover how Danielle gained "power over the group." Today Peter's journal was littered with questions, but he only received responses to the last one. When I asked the class what made them answer Peter's question, Bryan said, "Because he asked us." I had them listen carefully as Peter reread his entry. Again, they enthusiastically answered the last question. I asked why they didn't answer all Peter's questions.

Rodrick said, "That's the only one we know."

Again, I urged them to listen as Peter, happy to be the star of the show, read a third time. "Oh, it's because he looked up," yelled Alan. Peter then read once more, being careful to look up after each question. This time he received responses to all of his questions. Danielle read after Peter. She had once again written questions, and she looked up for responses after each one. I spotlighted question marks in a brief lesson after the sharing circle was complete. It is only a matter of time before Theresa and the other children attempt to write questions in their journals.

I have noted an increasing independence in Theresa as a reader and writer. She finished reading an old preprimer yesterday and told me that she needed to put it back on the shelf. As her contribution to our latest unit of study, she brought a cotton report and wanted me to read it. She told the class she got the information from a book. Most of the other children's reports had resulted from interviewing family members.

When Theresa's mom came to read with Roger and Tanya, I took a minute to ask her how Theresa came to write the report. She beamed, "Theresa told us she needed to find out about cotton. We searched the books at our house and at the neighbor's until we found something. Then she settled herself at the table and did her 'homework.'" Theresa bounced over as we talked, took her mother by the hand, and led her to the bulletin board covered with the children's cotton research. She pointed with pride to her report, held at an odd angle by a single strip of tape among the drawings, newspaper clippings, scraps of fabric, clothing labels, and crumpled written reports brought by her friends.

Cotton is the soft, white, stringy fiber of the cotton plant. Its most important use is in making cotton cloth.

Cotton is the soft, white, stringy fiber of the cotton plant. Its most important use is in making cotton cloth.

Theresa and Ethel both selected an old preprimer to share with me. Theresa said she chose it "Because it has ducks, and I took pictures of ducks." I invited them to practice together before reading to me. They giggled as they practiced, but they did practice. Theresa asked for help on *Lad* twice and *here* twice. After ten or so minutes of working together, Theresa read two stories successfully. Ethel chose to read only one.

OCTOBER 8

In *Approaching the Magic Hour*, Agnes Anderson describes a life of dedication and sacrifice so that the world might enjoy the gifts of her artist husband, Walter Anderson. It is the rogues who leave their imprint upon this world, and it is those who try to live in the realm of normalcy who contribute by bearing the suffering they cause. This room contains the elements of movers and shakers and those who will accept and bear their differences.

Will has so much potential, yet he insists on sharing it through only one medium, art. Walter Anderson followed his urge to compose in color and line, but he also valued language expression. Without his journals, we wouldn't realize what he was trying to say through art. He viewed art as we view language, as process rather than product. And, like James Britton, he viewed man as a participant rather than a spectator in nature. Will, even at age seven, is serious about his art. I will share this entry with him; perhaps I can speak to him about the value of written expression through Walter Anderson's art and journals.

OCTOBER 9

"A long time," rang the classroom chorus in response to my question about the amount of time to set for journal writing. I've set the timer for twelve minutes of writing. We read for twenty minutes and when I suggested that everyone find a stopping place in their reading, Alan complained, "But this is good. I want to read more." Then he turned a page and realized he'd read a whole book. "Hey, I read to the end … just one more page!" I've been concerned about the level of his engagement in reading and writing. These past few days show higher levels in both areas. He has revised his non-story from page after page of repetition to a story with a plot and action. I'll spotlight dialogue in his next book. Growth spurts in reading and in writing simultaneously … it seems natural that growth in both areas should go hand in hand.

I read from Glasser's *Control Theory in the Classroom* again. We all behave in ways that we believe will satisfy our needs for belonging, power, freedom, and fun. We have images, pictures, in our minds that dictate what we believe will satisfy these needs, and we can learn to choose the images on which our behavior is based. Certainly this classroom is set up to provide images of belonging for all the children — the compliment letters, the sharing circles, the learning groups. I hope the pictures they are forming focus on each of them as members of a community of readers and writers. Frank Smith says there is no evidence that anyone who wants to read cannot learn to do so. If internal motivation is the main ingredient, and if that motivation is dependent on a mental image of oneself as a reader, then my job is to provide an environment in which each child can form an image of self as reader.

Will's flashing Halloween watch just went off. Heads turn in unison to Will and then back to me. Dead silence. Will shrugs and says, "It just dropped." I lower my eyes and continue writing. So does Will. So do the others. Oh, how I value this time, this quiet reflective time for gathering my thoughts and for rejoicing in the children's eagerness to gather their own. The timer sounds and we all continue to write for several more minutes … Silence.

"Read over what you've written two or three times."

Katie erases. Ivan asks how to spell *like*, writes three words, and points with his eraser as he rereads several times. "How do you spell *diesel*?"

Writing/thinking continues. We've composed two collaborative writings about Christopher Columbus. The children copied the collaborative writing and added "extra" information independently. Yesterday, Peter added two pages; most children added at least two more sentences; Theresa did not add anything. Her hand flew up when I asked who planned to add to the writing today.

Theresa's extra information:

> *Better to go west*
> *'Oh,' said Christopher*
> *Columbus.*

Theresa was the first to read the Wright Group emergent reader, *Painters,* (my order was delayed and did not arrive until the second week of October). She makes excellent use of the picture clues in these books.

OCTOBER 10

"I want to get in groups," Will announced between the reading and writing phases of reading workshop. So the children shared their reading in groups rather than with partners. They have learned how to listen, to question, to respond, and to compliment others by working with partners. Now, in their learning groups, all that seems natural. Instead of monitoring their behavior, I can watch them interact and help each other learn. I watched Theresa hold her book to one side as if she were teaching while she told the other Tornados about it; I watched her sit on it and lean forward to hear what the other Tornados had to say about their books.

After they had talked about their reading in groups, I asked, "Why do you think I wanted you to talk about what you were reading?"

Danielle spoke first, "So we could tell the people in our group."

"So they would know," Lief added.

"No, so we would know," Peter corrected. His insights amaze me.

Roger grinned, "It came out of our heads."

During journaling time, Will grinned, winked at me, and silently held up his journal. He had drawn a detailed construction scene. Curvy arrows connected three explanatory sentences to illustrations of trucks and cranes. Theresa appeared to be copying from her book again. I remembered what a struggle I had allowing that to go on last year, after having forbidden it in years past. The children eventually came out of it last year, seemingly stronger writers for the experience. Copying familiar text into their journals seems to give some children the confidence they need to compose and write their own thoughts, so I have decided to let the copying continue a little longer this year, although there have been days when I've insisted that books be put away before journaling time.

We picked cotton in the cold this afternoon. Theresa's mother arranged our transportation. Theresa listened intently as the professor of entomology explained the life cycle of the boll weevil. Later, she picked two bags of cotton, singing "Jump down, turn around, pick a bale of cotton" with her classmates. The entomologist smiled as the children pretended to sweat, wiped their brows, and chanted, "It was hot. Oh my, it was hot. We picked and we picked and we picked and we picked." Peter and Bryan explained to him that they had learned the chant from Polly Greenberg's book, *Oh Lord, I Wish I Was a Buzzard.*

OCTOBER 11

The children's cotton knowledge covered the nine feet of bright pink chart paper I'd clipped over the chalkboard. Writing as fast as I could, I still missed some of the ideas they were calling out, but they recognized every missing idea and gladly, gleefully, repeated it. After thirty minutes of brainstorming, Katie and Kylie announced almost in unison, "I want to write my own." Others followed with requests to write independently. Yes! I congratulated myself silently for trusting the collaborative writing processes to lead to demands for independent writing opportunities. I love to hear them beg to write!

They had fun choosing the sentences and phrases they wanted from the chart paper. Some wrote three pages. Tanya needed help finding the ideas she wanted to copy into her report. Underlining her requests with a purple marker helped her find the words and phrases she needed. I did the same for others who couldn't find the ideas they wanted — purple underlines, green circles, brown boxes — I was happy to highlight whatever they needed. There is no reason for anyone to be left out of the writing experience when we go through prewriting and drafting processes as a large group and a selective revision process independently. Theresa narrowed her focus to boll weevils, copying two sentences and words describing the life cycle!

> Theresa   October 11
> We   learned   about boll
> weevils   eggs   larvae
> pupae
> adult
> They   kill   cotton.

OCTOBER 12

Yesterday Will wrote about boll weevils being enemies to cotton. He planned what he would write and told me about his plans. Then, after he wrote, he read his piece and, realizing he'd omitted two words, eagerly added them using a caret. Later in the day after I bought their cotton crops (illustrated fields with tiny fluffs of cotton glued on the plants), Will looked at the two pennies he'd earned and remarked, like a true farmer, "It ain't worth nothin'."

This morning I observed as the student teacher, Jennifer Tutor, conducted reading workshop. Theresa read for the entire fifteen minutes, leaning on her arms and very quietly mouthing the text of her book. Watching her compose in her journal, I remembered that she had copied from books for the past several days. Looking into space and mouthing words, she tapped the tip of the pencil against her chin, wrote, then repeated the sequence. When the timer sounded and the student teacher called the children to the sharing circle, Theresa remained in her chair, using a pencil as a pointer as she reread her entry. I heard the word "Mississippi" repeated as she practiced three times before joining the circle.

Usually I am a member of the sharing circle. Today I sat outside the circle, making notes about the sharing and interaction. Bryan read a lengthy update he'd written about the Bengals and the 49ers.

Rodrick read, "Oh, Lord, I wish I was a wolf."

Chris read so quietly we could barely hear him, "I read a book of science."

Emily held up a book, and as she did so she read aloud, "The little boy in this book was . . . ."

Natalie displayed a flower she'd fashioned from her cotton as she read, "I brought something to show." Her classmates crawled over for a closer look.

"It's a rose."

"It could be a brush."

"She could draw a boll weevil in front of it."

Tanya, the student teacher, and Darren passed. Ivan read an expansion of his entry from yesterday, "I like snakes and a cobra snake and a snake in the water and snakes in the tree."

Alan pulled a large pumpkin from its hiding place behind his back, "I like my pumpkin because it makes me wonderful."

Bryan responded, "That's the daddy of the other pumpkin, Alan. You can cut on it."

Orlicia held a pink teddy bear in her lap, "My bear's gonna help me read. I didn't like my book." Then she read a few lines of text she'd copied into her journal.

Peter had written a whole page. He read about half, skipped a series of math problems he'd written, then read an original writing about cotton.

Lief showed a picture and read the line he'd written above it, "The airplanes and the helicopters flew."

Will turned his journal sideways to show his illustration before reading the explanation he'd written to accompany it, "A helicopter can kick dirt. I like helicopters."

When it was her turn to share, Theresa read, "Did you know cotton grows in Mississippi?" She looked up as she finished reading and received lots of response to her question.

Rodrick noticed and said, "You looked up and everybody answered."

Feeling the need to point out to the class how Theresa had deliberately planned and used a question, I asked her to explain how she wrote her entry. She pointed to the first letter of her invented spelling for *grows* and said, "I almost put an l right here, but then I decided that I should put a *c* 'cause I sounded it out."

"What were you trying to do on this page?" I asked.

"I just wanted to put a question mark in my journal for the first time," was her matter-of-fact reply.

Did you know cotton
grows in Mississippi?

Note from Theresa's mother:

> *Theresa brought home some math papers that were incomplete and needed some help on them. They were addition facts. I introduced a short cut method of adding to her. She picked it up very quickly. She was very impressed with herself.*

Self-evaluation is difficult, even for adults.
But past experience has taught me that first graders
can learn to evaluate their own learning.
It's just that the starting point
almost always looks like a dead end.

October 16

Today Theresa copied words from her new crayon box and from a Wright Group book into her journal, drawing a horizontal line separating crayon box words from words copied from the book. Will announced in the sharing circle yesterday that he draws a horizontal line every time he starts to write about a new topic. Is the line a paragraphing device? In any event, Theresa and several other children appear to be relying heavily on copied text rather than composing original text in their journals. I decided to take them through an evaluation process which I hoped would lead them to discover the value of personal writing. (I believe there's a process for solving every problem!)

After the regular journaling phase of workshop was over, I asked the children to look back through their journals for evidence of their learning. "Turn the pages slowly. Look at your first journal entries and your later ones. Are they different? What do they show?" Self-evaluation is difficult, even for adults. But past experience has taught me that first graders can learn to evaluate their own learning. It's just that the starting point almost always looks like a dead end. The lively interaction that usually permeates my classroom was a long time coming. Most children haphazardly flipped through their journals. "I'm through," Roger announced. "I learned that I'm great." Others nodded in silent agreement.

"Look again," I pressed. "How can you tell you're great? How can you tell you are learning to read or to write better?"

Peter was the first to see growth. "I used to write only a few words; now I'm writing almost a whole page."

Bryan followed with, "Now I usually write a little about my book and a lot about what's on my mind. Before, I just wrote the name of my book and said that I read it, and I liked it." After five or six other children shared their discoveries, two things happened. First, all the children seemed to sense that identifying one's own growth was a satisfying pursuit; they began to look more closely at their journal entries. Secondly, those who hadn't been writing very much snapped to attention when others talked about writing whole pages. It seemed that they were making plans for showing some growth in that area!

Children met in learning groups, talking about their journals and their learning before writing evaluations about their learning. I wrote the word *evaluation* on the chalkboard and spelled *learned* for them. After that, they were on their own. In retrospect, I wish I'd stood at the chart paper and spelled every word they needed. I can't think of anything more important than the children's perceptions of their own growth, and Theresa's is one of several evaluations that I can't decipher.

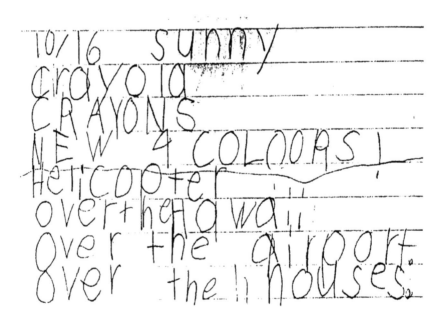

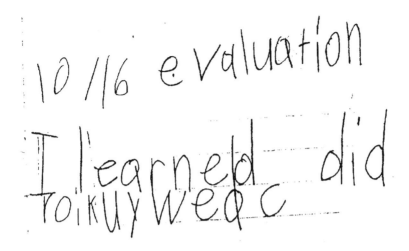

10 /16 evaluation
I learned did
To kuy wec

Note from Theresa's mother:

Oct. 17 Theresa came home with her Shared Reader. She was very proud! She read part of it to her dad who had been gone on a business trip for eight days and hadn't heard her read in a while. Before she started, she told her dad that she didn't know this book very well, so she wasn't good at reading it. She did very well. After a couple of stories, she wanted to stop. Her dad said, 'One more story.' She said, 'I can't read this one yet.' He persisted, and she read it. She did fine!

OCTOBER 18

As I wrote a rhyme on the board, Theresa asked why I put two *o's* in the word *too*. I taught a spotlight lesson (about three minutes) because of her comment. And Ethel concluded the lesson by adding, "If we want to write about the number two, we can just write a 2."

The rhyme was to be a cover sheet for a copy of a journal entry that the children chose to share with their parents. Several children wrote full pages about why they'd chosen their pages. About half the class explained their choice in one sentence. Theresa was one of five or six who did not write an explanation. Orally, she said, "Because it says I love my mom and dad." I told her that I especially liked it because the ideas on that page were all hers.

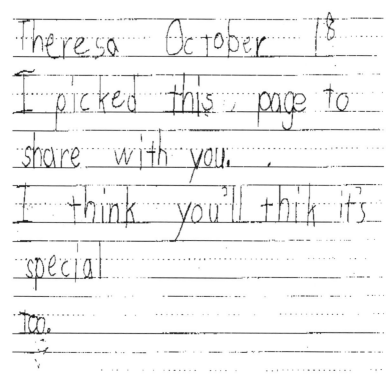

Theresa   October 18

I picked this page to

share with you.

I think you'll thik it's

special

Too.

Later Theresa chose to read her Star Watch Notebook to me, asking for help on *garage* and *wasn't*. She had recorded the position of the moon and stars for five nights in conjunction with our study of Christopher Columbus who "read the stars." She used repetition throughout the book to describe the moon, sometimes writing, "It wasn't out yet" and sometimes writing, "It was not out yet." We discussed the meaning of both forms and the differences between them. (Her mother had helped her spell both.) She went back to her seat with the assignment to highlight *wasn't* every time it appeared in her notebook. Shortly, she returned holding a bright yellow highlighter in one hand and a perfect completion of the assignment in the other. She accepted my invitation to gather up a few friends and teach them about *wasn't* and *was not*. Kylie, Ethel, Emily, Tanya, and Theresa settled in a corner behind the door, whispering, giggling, and highlighting *wasn't* in their booklets.

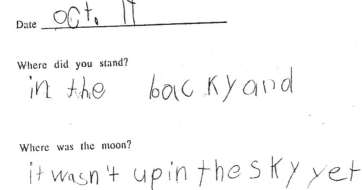

Date __OCt. 14__

Where did you stand?

in the backyard

Where was the moon?

it wasn't up in the sky yet

Where was the brightest star?

above my swingset

Note from Theresa's mother:

Theresa and I were studying together. We were reviewing addition. She said, 'Mom, I did this today when I was working with the student teacher.'

OCTOBER 19

We planned Ten Day as a day to celebrate and learn about the number ten. Each child brought ten similar items which we grouped and re-grouped throughout the day as we discovered various ways to define ten. Theresa brought ten toy ponies. I noticed that for each discovery activity, she followed the directions exactly. For example, when we were subtracting, I told the children to begin each scenario with all ten items on top of their desks, count out the exact number to be taken away and hidden in the "cave" beneath, and then count the ones that were left.

Theresa very carefully counted each time while some children used mental shortcuts and skipped some of the manipulations. However, on several occasions, she shouted the answer before completing the manipulations. She had a wonderful time using the ponies as counters, and she had confidence in her mental problem-solving abilities as well.

She showed me her journal entry for Ten Day. It says, "I brought math." She began *brought* with an *o* and *math* with a *c* but revised both words when I asked her to say the words and listen to the beginning sounds.

I brought math.

OCTOBER 22

Theresa came in late, in the middle of reading workshop. She'd had an upset stomach at home. Her mother says she believes it is something physical. If it is school-related, I don't know what could be the cause. At this moment, her head is down on her desk. Now it's up as she begins to write. I told her that since she'd missed reading time she could read during writing time, but she said she preferred to write.

OCTOBER 23

Indians … the children love to study about Native Americans, and I love reading from Clyde Bulla's book, *Squanto, Friend of the Pilgrims*. Before beginning the chapter for today, I asked for volunteers to retell the story. Then we role-played Squanto's mother crying and Squanto answering "Yes," to the invitation to travel with the white men. There was some discussion about how many times Squanto said "Yes." I reread the section in which he makes the decision to go to England as the children counted the number of times he said, "Yes." Theresa sat directly in front of me, carefully putting up a finger each time she heard the word.

As the children related to Squanto's decision to go on a short trip with the white men, all except Jereme enthusiastically raised their hands indicating they'd go. However, when Squanto was offered the chance to go to England without telling his mother good-bye, only half their hands went up. In the style of true indecision, Peter put his hand half way up, resting his forearm on the top of his head. "I just can't decide," he said.

Bryan had no doubts, "I would not leave my mommy."

I tried to help the children become aware of decisions in their own lives. After a large-group discussion, I invited the children to talk about decisions in their small groups. However, departing from the usual procedure, I did not give directions about who would talk first, second, and third. I simply told them that they had one minute to talk. I heard Orlicia telling the other Diesels about going to visit her aunt. I heard Will telling about his decision not to ride in a helicopter. I watched and listened as the Tornados spent the entire minute trying to decide who would tell about a decision first. Each of them had ideas about who should go first and why. After the timer sounded, I commented that I'd watched them and that they never got around to the assignment. Bryan grinned a defense, "But we were deciding."

Later, the children collaborated to write a short piece about Squanto. They were to copy and add to the story. Theresa's addition showed her interest in Squanto's decision to leave his mother and travel to England with the white men. She wrote "Yes" exactly four times as her extra information.

Orally, Theresa read *Helping*, a Wright Group emergent reader. She kept the meaning, but she made little use of initial sounds as she read the first time. *Knit* became *sew*. *Biscuits* became *cookies*. *Aunty* was read as *mom*. *Uncle* was read as *grandfather*. After she told the main idea of the story, I asked her to turn each page and together we looked at the wonderful substitutions she had made for all the words she didn't know. The emphasis here was on her talent for keeping the meaning of the story intact. On the second reading, the only missed, but self-corrected word was *uncle*, which she had first called *grandfather*.

OCTOBER 29

For magazine workshop, a variation of the reading workshop, Theresa chose to read the first issue of the class newspaper. The children had worked on the newspaper for two weeks, drafting independently and revising alone and in groups. Yesterday they received final copies, which we read in large and small groups and practiced reading independently. Theresa reported that she had read the camera article and the funny part to her family the night before.

As I observed her during the reading phase of the workshop, she pointed to words and read aloud softly. Occasionally she wrote and erased on the paper. I overheard her reading the children's favorite sentence, "Actually, this funny page could go on and on and on and on."

Our newspaper writing process helps the children synthesize what they've learned about a number of topics. Often, after we've worked on a class newspaper, I see leaps in the writing processes of individual children. James Moffett talks about setting up a field so strong that virtually whatever happens in it results in learning. I hope my classroom functions as such a field, and I'm sure it does when we're working on the newspapers.

For this issue, the children brainstormed possible topics, then each learning group chose one topic to write about. The Tornados chose to write about cameras. After talking in their groups, each child independently drafted information about the cameras. Mrs. Nail and I helped with spelling. As children wrote, they called out the words they needed, and we wrote them on chart paper. Theresa referred to the chart for *pictures* and *house*. She took a risk with *from*.

We took pictures from my house.

I took each group's first drafts, stacked them all together, called the children to the rug, and read the drafts, one by one. Other class members then had a chance to add information. This time, I jotted down their ideas. After school, I typed a combined "draft" that included everyone's information about every topic. I printed each draft on a separate page and made five copies of each page.

The next day I gathered the children on the rug and let them choose which articles they wanted to revise. I read the drafts aloud as they followed along. Then everyone went to work on the drafts while the assistant teacher and I circulated and responded to their ideas for changes. Occasionally, we'd announce a particularly good or interesting idea to the class: "Danielle thinks her sentence 'The wild baby is about the wolf licked Baby Ben and Baby Ben said Yuck' doesn't make sense. Has anyone worked on that one yet? Does anyone have an idea for making it better?" Sometimes, as in the case of Danielle's sentence, a child popped up with a solution which we shared with the class. We encouraged the children to confer with each other; Theresa worked with Emily and Kylie to revise two articles. She added information to the article about stars and changed sentences in the article about books.

Before school the next day, I combined everyone's revisions into a third draft, using double column format and making copies for each child. Again we read the entire newspaper together, noticing changes that had been made the day before. Katie had suggested that the word *I* didn't belong in our newspaper because, "We all wrote it and no one will know who that is." After our discussion, learning groups began working on final revisions. The Tornados worked together on the Camera article, but each child had an individual copy. Theresa concentrated on changing the pronouns *my* to *our* and *I* to *we*. (I enjoyed her side notes and arrows that related her family members to the terms used in the article. She's taking a leap!) Bryan drew arrows to rearrange sentences. Tanya watched

Theresa and Bryan and copied some of their marks onto her paper.

I typed these revisions into the final version of the newspaper. Children wrote the names of friends or relatives who would want a copy. We used calculators to find the total number of copies we'd need and figured the cost of ninety four-page papers at four cents per page. Children addressed copies to their friends in other classrooms and to relatives. Theresa sent copies to her grandparents in Iowa.

OCTOBER 30

The class transformed a pumpkin into a coach complete with a starry night background, lace curtains, and glittered pumpkin shell. A magical road covered in green cotton balls led to a three-dimensional castle. Theresa teamed with Kylie to construct the wheels for Cinderella's carriage. The wheels, Theresa explained, needed to be large in the back and smaller in the front. She and Kylie worked totally independently, finding large and small circular objects to serve as patterns for the wheels, designing the pattern of spokes for the wheels, and choosing the most glamorous colors of glitter. Theresa volunteered to bring six pretty ponies to pull the coach in the school pumpkin contest. As I was wrapping lace around Cinderella, I overheard Peter telling Orlicia, "Just put a *t*. I know it starts with *t*."

Peter is reading from the first newspaper now. "On and on and on and on," he reads. Just a few short weeks ago, I was concerned by his slow methodical word-by-word reading. Now I hear him reading jokes quietly with natural inflection and tone. Trust must be the overriding philosophy. Trust that if I provide an environment for language development, it will happen. Trust that the children will see themselves as members or potential members of this learning community. Trust that my observations and professional evaluations and judgments will help me guide these children into their own literacy.

OCTOBER 31

I observed as Jennifer conducted the reading workshop today. As the children rehearsed their journals prior to sharing in the circle I heard Rodrick reading aloud about his new crayons and his Ninja Turtle. One month ago, his journal pages were blank.

Ivan, in cap and glasses, read, "I like my book because it has a snake in it. I like snakes and I like books. I like Roger snake. I like Lief snake. I like Will snake. I like Rodrick snake and boy snake and girl snake."Alan pushed a photograph of two men with Mohawk haircuts into the center of the circle before reading, "I was reading about hair and it reminded me about my haircut."

Bryan had written a full page about Joe Montana and Jerry Rice, interspersed with comments and questions about his own athletic skills. Will had read and written about trains. His entry prompted a big discussion about what a diesel is. Ivan argued that a diesel is an engine. Will insisted that a diesel is a train. Lief called Theresa to attention three times. She'd been whispering to Kylie, who was her wheel-making partner for the Cinderella pumpkin project. Finally, Lief read, "Danielle is somebody, somebody ... " Peter fell over laughing before Lief could finish his poem.

When it was Theresa's turn to read, she called the name of almost every child, pretending to scold them to attention before she read. Peter lost patience with her, "Come on, you're wasting our time." Orlicia quietly asked her to go ahead and read. Theresa, after all the time spent calling everyone to attention, passed. Afterward, I could see her journal on the floor in front of her, the page filled with designs arranged in patterns across the page.

Note from Theresa's mother:

> *End of Oct. Have noticed a little break in progress. Her dad has been traveling a lot so there is less time for mom to spend individual time with Theresa. She still likes to read and does well although she questions her ability, saying things like, 'I can't read this story very well.'*

NOVEMBER 1

Yesterday I pulled old primers from the shelf and conducted a shared reading activity with a "scary" story called "They." I read the story first in an appropriately slow, deep voice. On several rereadings, I invited the children to join in as they felt comfortable reading. Then each child chose a favorite page and rehearsed it three times. Finally, the children used their deepest, scariest voices to read the favorite page to their response groups, receiving a pat on the back from group members afterward.

Theresa's journal entry today consisted of the text of her favorite page from that story. In the sharing circle, she read again, using a slow, deep voice. But this time she had the attention of the entire group, not just the Tornados! Suddenly, I realized one reason for children's copying of texts into their journals: perhaps they want the audience of the entire class to hear them read.

NOVEMBER 2

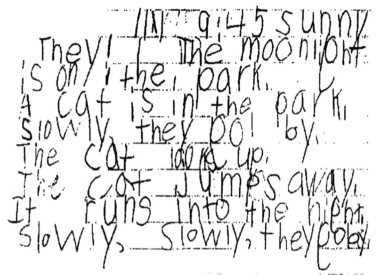

Theresa's interest in her family flowed into her journal again today. I feel like celebrating … on top of writing the longest original entry to date, she used correct initial consonants to invent spellings for *brother, sister,* and *named.*

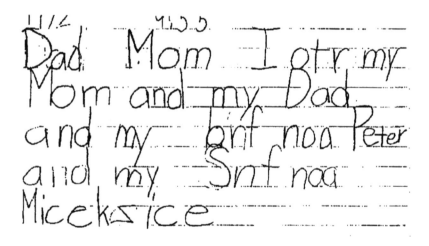

NOVEMBER 4

The most successful experience I've had lately occurred today during sharing time. We were on the rug a long time and the kids could have gotten tired, but they didn't. "Lief, read that again. I want to hear every word," Danielle said. Katie read her entry describing in detail how she and her mom had put up a poster she'd won the day before, mentioning how well the birds and moon in the poster matched her wallpaper. Bryan shared a full page he'd written about a conversation with his dad. Laquice shared her feelings about a story and told why she liked it. Charles wrote one sentence, and in it he asked a question for the first time.

November 5

This is an observation day for me because Jennifer is teaching. Watching and listening to the Ultimate Warriors as they talked about their books, I saw Rodrick scoot close to Darren and Peter and open the National Geographic magazine he'd been studying. "I've got a dog like that," he announced, pointing to a photograph.

"I've got a dog," Darren echoed.

Peter huddled closer, looking at the caption under a photograph, "That says 'Rodrick.'"

Rodrick wrinkled his nose and looked at me, "Does that say Rodrick?" The word was reckoning.

"You know how to spell your name. Does it?" I answered.

Rodrick shook his head and returned to his group.

Jennifer is showing confidence with the workshop approach. She's calling the children back to attention before giving any instructions. She's giving good guidance for journal writing, "Remember what you told your group members about your book. Remember the questions they asked. Who has already thought of something you didn't tell your group members? You can write all of that in your journal. Then write about whatever is on your mind." A few children are mumbling. Bryan has already begun writing. Jennifer says the magic words, "The timer is set." And there is quiet.

My thoughts wander to the math lesson Jennifer conducted yesterday. After reading *Where the Wild Things Are,* the children counted the 50 monsters they had drawn on strips of paper. Jennifer wrote the numerals as the children counted aloud, but they counted faster than she could write. I wonder if that means they are ready to write numbers to 100 independently? I also wonder if having them tell her how to write each numeral would have slowed them down and forced them to think about how numbers beyond 20 are written. (Write a 2 in the tens place and a 1 in the ones place for 21.) Of course, there's always the chance that the "telling" might have become noisy and chaotic. Teaching is constant adjusting based on *reading* the kids.

I wonder if Jennifer is sharing her journal with the children yet. It's hard to take the risks we ask students to take. They too sometimes feel vulnerable, or they would never pass.

The timer sounded; Jennifer remained quiet for a minute or so as children finished their entries. "Practice reading your journal aloud three times," she said, and the room was abuzz with children's voices. The oral rehearsal prepares them to read their own writing in the circle. Often it takes children naturally into revision processes. Orlicia ran straight to the rug. Darren sat, not reading. Kylie erased and rewrote. Ethel and Emily looked at Ethel's page and talked, then Ethel wrote again.

There was a great deal of noise on the rug. "Come on, Ethel," Jennifer called, and Ethel picked up her journal and headed for the rug. Danielle directed a comment to Orlicia who was holding a cotton ball behind her back, "Orlicia, you didn't bring something from home to show. That was already in the room. You didn't bring it."

The sharing began. Will showed a poster-like drawing. "This is gonna be a map. Starkville's police station. I'm drawing the inside of it. That's where I got my sheriff's badge. My uncle used to work there and he died just today. And I don't want anybody to bug me. I feel really bad today."

Bryan sympathized, "I felt bad when my granddaddy died." Bryan read about picking cotton and asked, "Do you want me to show you my journal page?"

Danielle shouted, "BRYAN! This is the first day you didn't write about baseball."

Bryan grinned, "Well, let me read this part right here." He read his reaction to a book that reminded him of a player for the 49ers. His classmates exchanged knowing looks; Bryan was talking sports again.

Danielle's red hair bounced, "I writed a poem about IT." (Has she connected the mystery of the story "They" to other pronouns?) Then she gave a list of clues about IT, one of which was that IT could fly.

Theresa asked, "Is IT a person?"

Danielle replied, "No, a person can't fly."

When it was Theresa's turn, she called several class members' names, getting full attention, before reading, "I brought something to show." She pulled a bright red belt from its hiding place behind her and glowed as her friends scrambled across the rug to experiment with it.

Darren said, "A strap … my mama got one of them." He took the belt, doubled it in half and demonstrated how to make it pop.

Several other children had a turn popping the belt before the student teacher scurried everyone back to their places in the circle. As Jereme tried to read his journal, Theresa took a turn with the belt. After several tries, she succeeded in making a big POP and was told by Jennifer to put it behind her. She grinned as she obeyed.

Theresa's entry is shown at the top of the next page. "I brought something to show" can be read easily. Her invented spellings include the three dominant consonant sounds in *brought*, the beginning sounds of *something* and *show*. She has command of the standard spelling for some words; she always capitalizes *I*, and here she's used *to* appropriately. Perhaps the 6x represents the size copied from the belt.

NOVEMBER 7

The children began drafting their first photography books today. Prior to this, they'd written about single photographs or illustrations. In this writing workshop, they collected all their pictures, categorized them according to topic and chose one category to be the basis for a book. In learning groups, they'd taken turns showing and elaborating on each photograph. Their glee filled the air with giggles and gasps and excitedly whispered questions and ideas sparked by the photographs.

Before the children began drafting, I shared my drafts of this manuscript, showing them the messy pages with arrows, strike-throughs, and misspellings. I asked them to tell how they would cope with words they could not spell. "Put down everything you hear," Danielle volunteered.

"Put the first letter, then other letters," Theresa suggested.

"Draw a line and put the letters you hear on it," Bryan offered.

Peter advised, "You can look around the room or in a book for some words."

Katie announced, "I need something that's on my 'I Can' poem." She scurried to the class *I Can* book and began flipping pages.

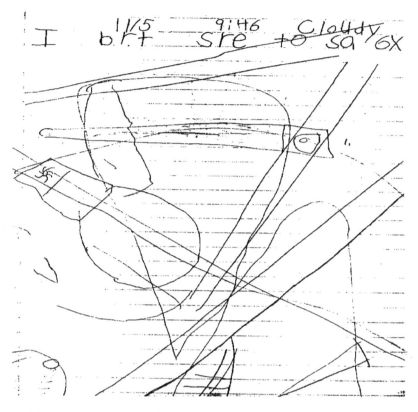

The prewriting time had been a noisy, idea-generating time, so before the drafting period began we discussed the need to be quiet so that ideas would not be interrupted. Each child, including Theresa, organized a personal "office" in which to work. Danielle and Emily had taught us how to make offices last week when they balanced open manila folders at each corner of their desks and arranged their pencils in paper cups. Their office idea caught on like wildfire, and it's wonderful for emphasizing independent working times. I noticed that Theresa had stacked books on top of her desk along with the writing folder that held her photographs.

Shortly after the drafting time began, she tiptoed to me, "You know what I do? If I need to write a word that is in my book, I just look in my book." She grinned and then returned to her seat. Two minutes later, she was holding a book and running her finger across the lines of print. After thirty minutes she had written a three-page draft and was ready to join a response group.

> *I was picking cotton. We were studying*
> *about the farm man.*
>
> *I was making a bird nest.*
> *Katie Nakeela*
>
> *I was making a M&M grid.*
> *I like to make a M&M grid.*
> *I like it.*

Since this was the first time the children had responded to writing in small groups, I combined two groups and joined in as a member. Theresa told her responders that she was writing about things that had happened at school. She showed photographs of herself picking cotton, making a grid to show how many of each color of M&Ms she had, and completing a chart with two friends. After she read her drafts about the three photographs, I asked her to try to identify the page she thought was best.

"This one," she said, holding up the page that showed the grid.

"Why do you think it's the best?" I asked.

"Because I wrote more," she replied.

"What do you need to do on these?" I asked.

"Write more," she answered.

Getting into the spirit of response, Bryan asked, "What were Nakeela and Katie drawing?"

"Oh, I have to go and ask them." Theresa scampered off, returning in less than a minute. "Nakeela drew a tent, and Katie drew a lantern."

Will gave his opinion, "I like the cotton the best. Are you gonna tell that we studied that?"

"Yes."

Jereme asked, "Why did you make an M&M grid?"

"Because I like to."

In an attempt to pull the responses together, I asked, "Do you know what you need to do, Theresa?"

"Yes, write more. That's why I was looking through … to see if I wanted more … to see if I wanted a period."

In the days that followed, Theresa used the writing workshop time to make revisions based on the responses of her group. Then she cut and glued the text onto heavy paper, taped the photographs on the pages, and sequenced her work. During a later conference, Theresa decided to write about two more photographs and add them to her book. "I think they got mixed up with the home group, but they should be with the school pictures," she explained.

Theresa deliberately included dialogue on one page because other children had made similar revisions to their books. She giggled as she told her plans to write "on and on and on," a phrase adapted from *Oh Lord, I Wish I Was a Buzzard.*

> *Emily said, 'Will you help me pick cotton?' I went on and on and on and on picking cotton for Emily.*

On another page, she tried to explain why she was using a ruler and why she had separated the M&Ms by color.

> *I was using a ruler to make an M&M grid. I separated the M&Ms so I could count the M&Ms.*

After she drafted the text, she underlined words for which she wanted correct spelling. These drafts, coupled with a recent journal entry, led me to think Theresa was ready for a brief lesson on the *ing* suffix. When I first asked her what she might need to add to *make* so that it would say *making* she grinned and put a *y*. In doing so, she gave a perfect example of overgeneralizing; in our daily journal headings, we had added a *y* to change sun to sunny, rain to rainy, and cloud to cloudy. Danielle joined us for a brief explanation of the *ing* ending. Theresa then saw a need to make the same change on another page. Her completed text follows.

> *I was picking cotton. We were studying about the farm man.*

> *Emily said, 'Will you help me pick cotton?' I went on and on and on and on picking cotton for Emily.*

I was making a bird nest.
Nakeela was making a tent.
Katie was making a lantern.

I was using a ruler to make an M&M
grid. I separated the M&M's so
I could count the M&Ms.

I was making a M&M grid.
I like to make a M&M grid.
I like everything at school.

Children learn by pretending.
As I gaze over this workshop scene
I wonder how many worlds are here.
How many princesses, pilots, and big hungry bears
inhabit the room?

NOVEMBER 8

Theresa read *Circus*, a Wright Group emergent reader to Mrs. Nail, who noted that she read it fluently. Although she didn't finish, Theresa showed her interest in the class study of bees with this journal entry. She's writing more. She's telling what she read and why she liked it. She's leaping again, becoming more independent as a writer. Her invented spellings are beginning to show awareness of blends (*st* in *stuff*) and final sounds (*fun, stuff, because, about*). Her separations of *about* (*a boat*) and *because* (*be kas*) also show awareness of syllabication. The spelling *yet* for *reading* indicates that she is not yet hearing /r/ and not hearing the *ing* ending.

NOVEMBER 9

Reading workshop took an alternate form today — geography workshop. Using small classroom atlases, we explored the physical and ethnographic plates together, the children's comments guiding our study.

"What other countries are colored green?" (for Germanic languages)

"This page shows where different colors of people live."

"I found the Atlantic Ocean."

"What page is it on?"

"Lots of pages."

"I found it!"

"Look at these brown parts. Those are mountains."

"Hey, here's another ocean. It says 'Indian,' Indian Ocean?"

"Is this England?"

"I found London."

Theresa started a search for familiar places in the United States when she announced, "I found Iowa. I was born there. My cousins live there."

"Here's Texas. I used to live there."

"I found Mississippi three times."

"I found San Francisco. The 49ers live there, and once there was an earthquake there during the World Series."

As I set the timer for journal time, Roger asked that the word "found" be written on the board so he could write about all the places he found in the atlas. I noticed that most children copied the names of familiar locations, then began copying names of places that were unfamiliar to them.

During sharing time, the impact of geography on our lives became apparent as children read about finding cities they had visited, places where wolves live, countries mentioned in the many books we've shared, and Middle Eastern countries seen nightly on the news. Theresa, along with several others, listed the names of a few familiar and numerous unfamiliar points on the globe. When I suggested that the children draw one line through the names of places they did not know about, Theresa crossed out all except London, which she knew was Squanto's adopted home. She had evaluated her own knowledge of the world!

Later, children used their journal entries as first drafts to compose a paper for the school's celebration of Geography Week. After expanding the ideas from their journals, the children met in their response groups, added more ideas, and helped each other find words that were not correctly spelled. In individual conferences, the assistant teacher and I provided correct spellings on stickie notes and helped children place capital letters and periods. Theresa's journal entry and subsequent published writing follow.

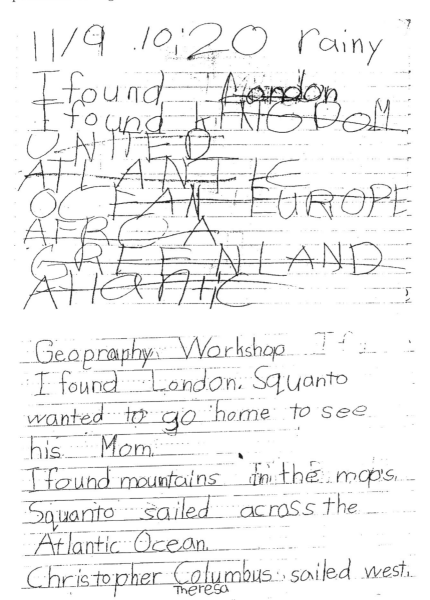

11/9 .10:20 rainy

I found London
I found KINGDOM
UNITED
ATLANTIC
OCEAN EUROPE
AFRICA
GREENLAND
ATLANTIC

Geopraphy Workshop I
I found London. Squanto
wanted to go home to see
his Mom.
I found mountains in the maps.
Squanto sailed across the
Atlantic Ocean.
Christopher Columbus sailed west.
Theresa

NOVEMBER 12

We've begun writing formula poems to celebrate each class member. Yesterday we wrote about Danielle and, in the process, discovered the concept of agreement. The children brainstormed words to tell what Danielle likes to do. I wrote them on chart paper, and Danielle chose three for her poem. We repeated the process for a sentence about Danielle. Our first draft read:

> *Danielle*
> *smile*
> *dance*
> *play*
> *She writes in her office.*

Danielle said, "We need to put an *s* on *smile* and *dance* and *play*." "Why?" I asked.
Danielle explained, "It will sound better with *writes*."
Today, writing about Bryan, we examined the meaning of the word *compromise*. All the children agreed to include sports words as the first three lines, but they also wanted to use the word *actually* (they remember it from their favorite sentence in the class newspaper). There was some discussion about just where to add the word and they practiced reading it in numerous positions, finally *compromising* on this final sentence:

> *Actually, he always writes on and on and on and on about*
> *baseball and football.*

During reading workshop Theresa read first from her bedtime story book. The second time I glanced up, she was pointing to words in *The Teeny Tiny Woman*, and the third time she appeared to be reading the pumpkin book she wrote about Halloween. Oh, yes, I noticed the drop in noise level this morning during reading time. It came after four or five minutes. I have my artist friend, Susan Dorsey, to thank for teaching me about noise level as an indicator of engagement. She says that it takes a while for artists to become fully engaged in their work. A studio session will begin with lots of talk and some laughter, but as the artists become engaged, as the right brain kicks in with insights and connections, the noise level in the studio drops noticeably. It happens in reading work-shop, too, sometimes. The children almost always start out reading loudly, aware of potential audiences all around them. But when they become engrossed in their reading, the voices drop. I can hear the drop sometimes on magical days when there are no interruptions from visitors or speaker systems, on days when we are real readers. Usually, the drop comes after eight or nine minutes. Today, after five!

When volunteers told about the books they'd read, Theresa looked at each person who shared and listened intently. She seldom raises her hand, but she usually has something to say when I call on her. When I invited her to tell about her reading this morning, she said, "Well this old woman took a bone that didn't belong to her, and a voice kept saying 'Give me my bone!'"

As I look around the room, I see that Theresa is referring to *The Teeny Tiny Woman* as she writes in her journal. Bryan has written half a page, Peter almost as much. Peter seems relaxed about writing, occasionally glancing up. Bryan focuses solely on his task, his nose barely four inches from the page as he writes. Will's page is covered with color. (Didn't I make a rule about using markers and crayons in journals?)

"Read your journal entry three times out loud." These standard instructions for rehearsal before reading in the sharing circle serve different purposes for each child. Today Bryan paused his rehearsal to add quotation marks. Theresa erased. Roger read loudly. Emily flipped open a book and compared a standard spelling letter by letter to her invented spelling. Katie, who had watched Charles draw in his journal, yelled, "Charles, may we see your pretty picture?"

NOVEMBER 13

At our reading conference today, Theresa retold a story with a detailed sequence of four events. Then, using her finger as a pointer, she read with fair expression. She immediately self-corrected after reading *went* as *was*.

She introduced the bee report she'd copied at home with this journal entry which she read in the sharing circle before showing her report.

> *I got something to show.*
> *It is a bee fact.*
> *Bees are insects.*

11/13 sanny 9:30
I kot seto cot
It is a bee fog
bees are in sects.

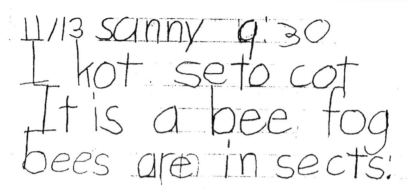

Bees are in sects.
We need bees.
A bee carries
seeds from
one flower to
another. The
bees sting
protects it.

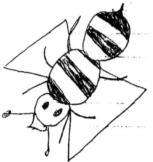

Note from Theresa's mother:

Nov. 13 Has been picking up books at home to read. Took one to school to read to Mrs. Swain, 'Monkey and the Bee.'

NOVEMBER 14

For our "Author's Workshop," children created a display of all the books they've published by lining them up along the chalk tray. I distributed small pads of stickie notes, and the Room 9 book reviewers went to work reading their classmates' books and leaving complimentary notes inside the front covers. Theresa's book, *What Goes on at School*, received four notes. Orlicia wrote, "Theresa, I like when you said what goes on at school. I like when you said on and on for Emily." Peter wrote, "Theresa, I like the part where you said I am making a grid." Theresa attached notes inside two classmates' books. At the conclusion of the peer evaluation activity, every child had two to four notes that pointed out specific strengths of his or her book.

In our reading conference, Theresa wanted to show me how she could read *Wheel on the Chimney*, a library book which, she explained, "My mom's been teaching me but I keep on forgetting because it's hard." She read the first two sentences of the book, then we discussed the pictures and content of the story as she turned the pages. The last page repeated one of the sentences she'd learned to read. I invited her to read it, and she did, even though it was not lined in the same arrangement as on the first page. Theresa opted to observe an insect collection during journaling time. She copied labels from the collection to compose her entry.

11/14   9:15 Sunny
Monarch Praying Ma'e Mant's
Cricket Grasshopper
Spur Throated grasshopper

NOVEMBER 15

Wiggle, wiggle, wiggle. The children are taking longer than usual to settle into their journal time. The district superintendent stepped into our classroom while we were reading this morning. I can't believe I motioned for him to be quiet, but if I let adults disturb their reading, the children will think that it's not important. Besides, he understands the value of adult models for reading; I'm exquisitely fortunate to have administrative support at every level.

Theresa tugged on my skirt between the reading and writing phases of workshop this morning. She pointed to the gerbils who have been living in our classroom for about a week. "You know those animals over there? They're cuddling." After overhearing Theresa's conversation about the gerbils, Tanya and Roger also talked about the animals cuddling.

Peter announced that he didn't feel like writing in his journal. I told him he could continue reading, but I see that he's writing. He chose an atlas to read today; I can see the first line of his entry, "I found where Squanto lived. You just find New York and it's right under there."

For a month or so, I've offered three or four children per day the option of observing and writing "field notes" instead of writing the usual journal entry. The gerbil cage is one observation station. Danielle began to cry this morning when she saw Kylie getting another turn at the gerbil station. She and Kylie are there together now. I thought Will would jump at the chance to sit on the bench outside the principal's office and record the goings and comings of children and adults. Katie and Orlicia recorded bits of overheard conversation that had everyone laughing earlier in the week. I was wrong; Will chose not to observe the office. He seemed hesitant to accept the responsibility I attached to the privilege, "You'll have to sit quietly to observe and write. You can't talk to people you see."

Will said, "I'd better just write like usual in my journal."

I had to move Charles during workshop. He was just sharing his delight in *Love You Forever* but he disturbed Jereme, Danielle, Ivan, and me with his poking and pointing and giggling. He's sitting in a chair on the rug now, reading to himself.

The timer sounds. Rodrick grins ear to ear and holds up his journal for me to see. Yesterday I told him I was disappointed that he'd spent precious, valuable writing time scribbling. Today, he has filled a page with writing; his letters are huge, but it's meaningful WRITING.

Theresa's journal entry illustrates her use of questions to elicit response from her classmates.

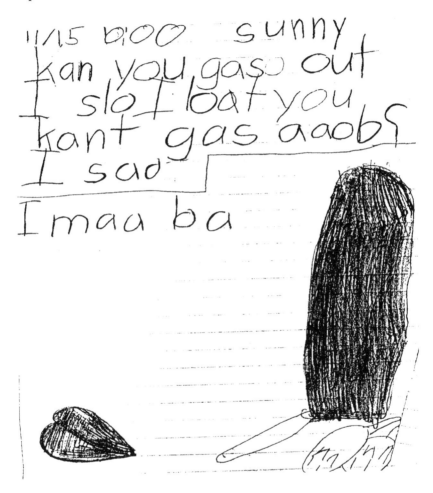

*Can you guess what
I saw? I bet you
can't guess about
(what) I saw.*

NOVEMBER 20

Orlicia's voice dominates the rumble of reading workshop, "Tromp, Tromp, Tromp! Who's that tromping over my bridge?"

Alan leans over and points to a picture in Kelley's book, "That's really Miss Nelson," he says.

Laquice reads *Jamberry* with a stern expression on her face and a ruler in her hand. I wonder if she's playing school, and, if so, I hope she's modeling a teacher seen on television!

Children learn by pretending. As I gaze over this workshop scene, I wonder how many worlds are here. How many princesses, pilots, and big hungry bears inhabit the room?

Kylie's light, high-pitched voice squeaks out a story. "I need some hair, too." "Take all you want."

Rodrick turns to Will's desk. Peter counts the words on a poster, twists and turns, then rests his head on a shoe box on his desk. What's in the box?

The options for journaling grow. This morning the children might write about their reading ... how they feel about it, what it reminds them of, about posters I brought them from the National Council of Teachers of English convention, or about ideas for poems on Will and Theresa. My curiosity about pretending prompted still another option. I asked them to write explaining what, if anything, they were pretending while they were reading. My theory is that pretending is integral to their learning processes. Vygotsky says that emerging literacy development lies in a zone of proximal development, that what children are ready to learn lies just beyond what they already understand, where knowledge and curiosity meet.

I'm wondering just what role pretending may play in that development and what it means for instruction. In the reading act, children might pretend to take on the voice of a character, to present to an audience, to read the text by inventing a script. I see this so often with children who are on the edge of reading. Their invented script sounds like "book language," not like "talk" about the pictures. They learn to differentiate between spoken language and the rhythm of print somewhere along the road to literacy. I can hear it in their interpretations of books right before they are ready for "real" reading.

Are there children who don't pretend? How is pretending literacy different from pretending to drive a car or pretending to parent? How is pretending literacy different from pretending fantasies like Superman and Ninja Turtles? Can all pretending be lumped together? Is pretending literacy different? Is it possible to pretend literacy? Is the very act of "pretending" to read or write an actual engagement in literacy? Charles has broken through the wall. He's been pretending to read his journal all year. This week I can read his journal and so can he!

NOVEMBER 26

Theresa read from an anthology she brought from home. She told me it was an easy book and read fluently without using her finger. She used little expression, but the stories themselves were devoid of expression, most of them based on the use of phonograms.

Theresa wrote about her ballgame meeting with Bryan, the class expert on sports. She used invented spelling so expertly that I had no difficulty reading it. Upon reading it to me, she said, "Oh, I need a period there and there." What progress she's made since September! Her mother and I had a wonderful time this afternoon, poring over her semester work folder and journal entries.

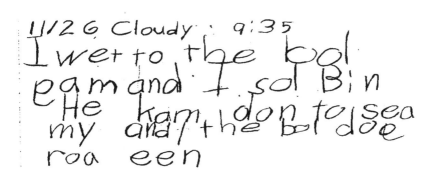

*I went to the ball
game and I saw Bryan.
He came down to see
me and the bulldogs
were winning.*

NOVEMBER 28

This morning I observed as Jennifer led the children in writing a formula poem about Tanya. I listened as the children first collaborated to write a list of things Tanya can do. Roger, Ivan, Peter, Kylie and others reminded the class regularly that each word (verb) needed an *s*. I listened, amazed, as Tanya announced that she could spell *participate*. And she did, all except for a couple of letters. A few weeks ago, Tanya didn't know one letter from another. She learned as she wrote about her classmates.

NOVEMBER 30

Will cupped his hands and delivered a warm whisper into my ear, "Look on your desk. I brought something for you. I made the top and the bottom and all of it for you." It was an exquisite silver and white pipe cleaner sleigh with a red Hershey wrapper seat. The runners on the sleigh were double tracks of bent pipe cleaners that curled up in front. A blue clay reindeer had a harness around its neck and well-shaped muscular legs; the back leg even had thick thighs. The left front leg of the reindeer was raised as if it were prancing. Will beamed, "That's a horse, not a deer. That's supposed to be snow on the edge of it." He pointed to fat white pipe cleaners placed on the upper surfaces of the sleigh. Will's classmates crowded around him. Inspired by his work, Theresa asked if she might look through our art supplies for pipe cleaners.

We celebrated Roger this morning. As the class began brainstorming for the poem, Theresa said, "We might have to change something." The children are learning about revision as they learn to write. It saddens me that some elementary teachers don't realize that revision is at the heart of the thinking process. How many times have I heard first-grade teachers say that revision is for the upper grades?

After the student teacher read the Indian story, "Little Ugly Face," Will announced, "That's just like Cinderella." The student teacher reached for a marker and chart paper to capture the children's quickly unfolding ideas about the similarities of the two stories.

Katie said, "They both have mean sisters."

Emily added, "They both went to a party."

"Well, not really," Peter explained, "Cinderella went to a ball and Little Ugly Face went to a feast."

Theresa smiled, "Cinderella got a beautiful dress, and Little Ugly Face got a pretty blanket."

During our reading conference, Theresa read *Jesse Bear, What Will You Wear?* with lovely expression. She named the characters and explained that the main idea of the book is, "He kept wearing different things all day."

*Much of what we write has been
in our minds and hearts for a lifetime.
But as teachers, we must provide ways
for children to call up these experiences.*

December 1

Frank Smith's book, *Essays Into Literacy,* is so packed with truths that I find new ones every time I read it. What will be read quickly can be written slowly. How true of my writing. I find myself laboring more over a 10-line business letter than over a page of a research paper. What makes the difference? The research paper will be graded. The business letter needs to secure money. The research paper can be as lengthy as I like. If I don't get it all said on one page, I can write another. The business letter must be short. The lines must be packed. So I work and stew over the 10-line letter, choosing words, packing sentences. I add to the research paper. I say in 60 pages what might have been trimmed to 45 had I tried.

Children need their writing done for them until they can write for themselves. I needed to read that again after reading Cambourne's book, *The Whole Story,* in which he makes a case for insisting on approximations in spelling before providing help. Cambourne and Smith are both right. It's my job to decide when Charles or Ethel is ready to approximate on paper, when and how swiftly to move from dictation to independent drafting.

Smith is right about prewriting, too. Much of what we write has been in our minds and hearts for a lifetime. But as teachers, we must provide ways for children to call up these experiences. Soon I'll lead the children to write about their own special family traditions. The prewriting activities to help them remember family events need to include some modeling, lots of talking, drawing, and interviewing parents.

DECEMBER 4

I read several books by Ezra Jack Keats during shared reading time this morning. Then the children each chose a title to work on. Our school library has multiple copies of all the titles, so children who've chosen the same book can work together on it. All these children feel successful as readers. There are no bluebirds or redbirds. Anyone who wants to work on *Goggles* can. I don't know of a better way to show high expectations for every child than to make all the shared books available to everyone. If Charles has trouble learning to read the entire *Goggles* book, he can choose one or two pages to learn to read like an expert.

Some children chose to read their Keats books during workshop time; others retreated into old favorites. I overheard someone reading *Goggles*. I was immersed in *I and Thou* by Martin Buber, but I glanced up when I heard the noise level drop ... eleven minutes, longer than usual. At the conclusion of reading time, Peter, holding a science book open, said, "My dad says he'll get me some wires so I can make this."

Orlicia looked at me, "You're gonna love this rhyme I found. Listen to the last line, 'Whether you are a *he* or a *she*.'"

Charles, flipped to the front and back of *Brown Bear, What Do You See?* and announced, "This is a circle book." (He's found the identical fly leaves in the front and back and has overgeneralized to assume that graphics rather than story content make a "circle" book.)

Bryan read a full page he'd written about Monday night football. Emily read an account of a stranger coming to her house the night before. Will wrote about the troops in Saudi Arabia. Katie wrote a full page about *Goggles*. Theresa read from her journal, "I was the (line) leader yesterday. It was fun being a leader because you don't have to stop (at the door) at lunch." A fire drill interrupted our journal sharing time. We left our journals on the rug and filed outdoors with other classes.

Outside, Roger fretted, "It's gonna burn up our journals!"

DECEMBER 6

In response groups, the children have selected one story to present to the class. They practiced reading until all members of the group had successfully read the story. ("Do not give help unless it is asked for. If you want help, ask or spell out the word you need.") The system worked well; I sat nearby and noted the skill and patience and interest the children took in each other's learning. Then they decided on a method of presentation and began to work on visual aids for their shows. The Tornados are making stick puppets from poster board and popsicle sticks.

DECEMBER 7

The children wanted to write a class book about the gerbil that's been loose in our room for a couple of weeks. It has destroyed one package of tissue paper, eaten the corners of the children's displayed work, chewed the record player cord in several places, and left trails of shredded paper and droppings throughout the classroom. As I handed out paper, Will's hand went up: "Don't anybody write that it bit my finger because I'm going to write that. It WAS MY finger."

Theresa grinned, "It will probably eat our book."

I asked, "Are you going to write that?"

Theresa said, "Yes, and nobody else can." Later, after all the children had a draft, we met in the sharing circle to read them. As they read, they discussed the bad gerbil. Several left the circle to make revisions and returned with new information. Orlicia suggested that we make a hall display to share our bad gerbil experiences: The Gerbil That Ate Room 9. I suggested they return to their seats and lightly mark words they'd like to have spelled correctly. I wrote the words on the board as they called them out. As a class, we checked for capital letters, periods, and question marks. It's marvelous that sentence fragments are not a problem; these children make poems out of them.

DECEMBER 10

Note from Theresa's mother.

> *Wow! did Theresa ever read GREAT tonight! Her fluency was so good. She tried to sound out words before she asked [for help] from her library book ... words like cackles, squawk, jabber, ribbing ... words that were new to her. Up to now, she would look at a word, see she didn't know it, and ask for help. I know, from your notes at the beginning of the year, not to force her to sound out words and lose*

the meaning of the sentence. But this definitely seems to be another major step in her learning. Her dad and I greatly appreciate your direction in her learning this year. She (as well as her dad and I) is definitely learning HOW THERESA LEARNS!

DECEMBER 11

This semester is drawing to a close. In half a school year, Theresa and her classmates have grown into a community of readers and writers. In her family traditions story, Theresa showed her ability to sustain a subject, to add details to make the story interesting to her readers, and to use standard and invented spelling to convey her message. With advice from her response group, she revised this piece until she and her group members were happy with it. I am elated.

> The Christmas tradion in
> my family is I pow to irw and I see
> my grandpa and grandma and cousins
> a I eat pod fad. I play
> with the Christmas tree. They have
> ofns and the haws of mre
> cost. My cousins play wt the Mary
> and ost. I po tothe sken polsa
> and go sken. It is fon.
> My Mom helps me ske and smttimes
> I fall. My Mom pichs me up. There
> is a big hill. Ifl and my shis
> fall off.

December 12
Note from Theresa's mother.

>*Theresa wrote a letter to Santa last night. This is how it went:*
>*Sata will you kam to my aos be for I go to iow?*
>*Ples kam 19. thak you. Theresa*
>*As you can see, she wrote it herself. Her father and I are very impressed and pleased!*

REFLECTIONS

As I think about this semester with Theresa, I think about Shakespeare's line, "The world is a stage ..." Our classroom scene is drama come to life. Theresa and the other children are the writers and players; I'm the director of lighting. Each changing scene is a whole event, filled with the stuff of language and life. The children help create the scene, and I help them find what they need in it to continue growing Sometimes the entire stage is lit, and each child gravitates to the most personally satisfying part. Other times, I narrow the spotlight to focus every child's attention on a concept of language or life. Many times, in reading and writing conferences, I spotlight different language elements, depending on the needs of each child. Theresa contributes to the whole drama while she pulls from it the confidence and experiences she needs to become a reader and writer.

The partnership with Theresa's parents has had a ripple effect on my teaching. Reading the notes from her mother gave me a window into Theresa's learning that I wanted to experience with every student. But how could I initiate a written dialogue with all the parents? It seemed that the first step was to bring the parents together and share something of myself with them, to let them know the depth of my concern and respect for their children, to create a nonthreatening environment in which they would be willing to share with me ... not private family secrets, but information that would help me understand the children as learners. I began with a parent workshop that has since grown into a series of workshops where parents come to the classroom, without their children, for evenings of talking, writing, and sharing with each other and with me.

At the first workshop all but five children had at least one parent present. It was a magical time. First I had each parent fill out a name card with information about their child on it. Parents used the name cards as a basis for conversation as they moved around the classroom commenting on and asking questions about the information on each other's cards. The laughter was loud. The Episcopal priest had a great story about the funniest thing his child had ever said. Charles's grandmother was right in there cracking everyone up with her grandson's eating habits. The priest, the maid, the housewife, the artist, the teacher, the accountant, the

Burger King counter clerk all came together as extended members of our classroom community.

After the whole group brainstormed the needs of first-graders, we reviewed the list and marked those that should be met by teachers and those to be met by parents. You've already guessed that both should provide everything on the list ... including the snacks that Charles's grandmother talked about. Both should love, hug, praise, discipline, set limits, guide, offer one-to-one attention ...

In pairs again, they pretended their partners were me and told "me" what I really needed to know about their children, their special needs and how to meet them. The room roared with "Sherry, you need to know that ... " When I asked them to spend ten minutes in total silence writing a letter to me about their children, they reached for the paper and began writing before I could finish my I-don't-care-where-you-put-your-commas speech. Every single parent gave me their letters that night, and they are wonderful pieces of a dialogue that promises to continue all year.

But what about my communication with the parents? I can't write a case study about every child. True, but I can write narrative evaluations in which I cite specific work samples as evidence of learning. I pull accounts of interactions from my journals. I tell about the child's contributions to lessons or class discussions. And I quote from the child's literacy folder (where I record reading and writing conferences) and his or her portfolio. Each parent now gets a one- or two-page reflection on progress with suggested directions for future learning twice each year. Most respond with equally lengthy reports of the progress they're seeing at home. I'd always known that contact with parents was important. Theresa and her parents showed me the power of real parent involvement.

BIBLIOGRAPHY

References

Anderson, A. (1989). *Approaching the magic hour*. Jackson, MS: University Press.

Atwell, N. (1987). *In the middle*. Portsmouth: Boynton Cook.

Britton, J. (1986). *Language and learning*. New York: Viking Penguin.

Buber, M. (1958). *I and Thou* (R. G. Smith, Trans.). New York: Collier Books, Macmillan.

Cambourne, B. (1988). *The whole story: Natural learning and the acquisition of literacy in the classroom*. New York: Scholastic, Inc.

Cutting, B. & Milligan, J.L. (1990). Learning to read in New Zealand. *Teaching K-8*, Aug./Sept., 62-65.

Glasser, W. (1986). *Control theory in the classroom*. New York: Harper & Row.

Katz, L. G. & Chard, S. C. (1989). *Engaging children's minds: the project approach*. Norwood, NJ: Ablex Publishing Corporation.

Katz, L. G. & Chard, S. C. (1989). *Engaging children's minds: The project approach*. Norwood, New Jersey: Ablex Publishing Corporation.

Leigh, L. (1990). The big backyard. In *Mississippi primary language arts curriculum*. Jackson, MS: Mississippi State Department of Education.

Smith, F. (1983). *Essays into literacy*. Portsmouth: Heinemann.

Smith, F. (1988). *Insult to intelligence: The bureaucratic invasion of our classrooms*. Portsmouth, NH: Heinemann.

Vygotsky, L. S. 1978. *Mind in society.* Cambridge, Mass.: Harvard University Press.

Children's Literature

Brown, M. W. (1954). *Wheel on the chimney.* Philadelphia: Lippincott.

Bulla, C. (1974). *Squanto, friend of the pilgrims.* New York: Scholastic.

Cooper, E. K. (1979). They. In *Sun and shadow* (M. Early, ed.). New York: Harcourt Brace Jovanovich.

Crews, D. (1982). *Harbors.* New York: Macmillan.

Carlstrom, N. W. (1986). *Jesse Bear, what will you wear?* New York: Scholastic.

Degan, B. (1983). *Jamberry.* New York: Harper & Row.

Dodds, S. (1987). *Elizabeth Hen.* New York: Macmillan.

Early, M. ed. (1979). *Sun up.* New York: Harcourt Brace Jovanovich.

Frost, M. (1991). *Circus.* Bothell, WA: Wright Group.

Galdon, P. (1984). *Teeny tiny woman.* New York: Clarion.

Greenberg, P. (1968) *Oh Lord, I wish I was a buzzard.* New York: Macmillan.

Hucklesby, H. (1989). *This little piggy.* Bothell, WA: Wright Group.

Jacobs, L. B. (1971). Monkey and the Bee in *The read-it-yourself storybook.* New York: Golden Book.

Keats, E. J.(1969). *Goggles.* New York: Macmillan.

Martin, B., (1983). *Brown Bear, Brown Bear, what do you see?* New York: Holt, Rinehart & Winston.

Munsch, R. (1986). *Love you forever.* Willowdale, Ontario: Firefly.

Sendak, M. (1963). *Where the wild things are.* New York: Harper & Row.

Taylor, S. (1989). *Helping.* Bothell, WA: Wright Group.

Wagstaff, A. (1989). *Make a face.* Bothell, WA: Wright Group.

Williams, R. (1990). *Painters.* Bothell, WA: Wright Group.

Williams, S. (1989). *I went walking.* Gulliver.

About the Author

Sherry Swain, a classroom teacher for Starkville Public Schools, is Director of the Mississippi State University Writing/Thinking Project. She has conducted numerous professional development and retreat sessions for teachers and administrators. An avid classroom researcher, she has investigated vocabulary development, writing/reading process, the effects of the writing process on self-esteem, and portfolio assessment. Areas of interest include the teaching of writing, writing as a learning tool, emergent literacy, at-risk students, authentic assessment, and professional development for teachers. She and her husband are the parents of two daughters.